MW01630467
Make your home Sparkle and Shine!

ALSO BY STEPHEN BROWN

Glitterville's Handmade Halloween

Glitter Ville's HANDMADE CHRISTMAS

A GLITTERED GUIDE FOR WHIMSICAL CRAFTING

Stephen Brown

Andrews McMeel
Publishing
Kansas City • Sydney • London

Bryan "Chico" Crabtree
Above all, I must thank my friend Bryan for his fabulous photography and full-time devotion in helping me create this book . . . and for making every day seem like Christmas!
Acknowledgments
Coleen O'Shea
A true gift among literary agents, who always brings her patience to the party!
To Our Andrews McMeel Team...
Grace Suh
Christi Hoffman
Holly Ogden
Tamara Haus
Susan Wilson
Sandra Herrera
Mary Kate Cofer
Myra & Larry Green
Jonathan Crouch
Ann Knight
Marianne Custer
Lynn Shepherd
Dolly Pauld
Janis Johnson
Laurel McCall
David Dorsey
Ann Baker
Mark Howard
Angela Bynum
Making every day a holiday takes more than just glitter and glue,
but how it all happens most have not a clue
that there are lots of enablers behind "Make & Do!"
Special thanks to all my friends who have made Glitterville a part of their lives over the years—even when that little voice inside of them clearly said, "Run!"

Contents

Happy Holidays
Jeff, Karen & Aaron Crabtree
Anne Powers
Anita Donofrio
Bill Black
Katie Wood
Mom, Dad & Mike!
Nana & Papaw

Introduction

For me, the magic and excitement of the Christmas season has always been more about the weeks and days leading up to the long-awaited holiday's arrival than the actual day itself. I love all the preparation and presentation the holiday season brings, so much so that when the actual day arrives, it's a bit of a letdown because I know that all the make-and-do madness will soon come to an end. But just because it's not Christmas on the calendar doesn't mean it can't be "Crafts-mas" every day of the year!

Although the activities in this book are all designed to make your home sparkle and shine for the holidays, the materials and techniques used to create them can be applied to making anything your mind can imagine! And because I don't believe your creativity should ever be limited by the number of expensive craft supplies you can afford, all of my projects are made from easily acquired basic materials (you'll find them discussed in the Glitter Guide on page viii)!

Crafting Christmas memories can be fun for the whole family, no matter the age. If a project seems too difficult for the very young, just simplify it to their current skill level, or show them the picture and let them make it their own way . . . it's OK! That's the beauty of creating. There is no right or wrong!

Each December when I unwrap boxes of my handmade decorations, it's like seeing old friends with whom I can remember the joys of Christmases past. . . . And they know, because they were there, too!

And that is my Glittered Wish for YOU!

Stephen Brown's
Glitter Guide
A Manual for Make and Do!
Mastering the art of Make and Do means learning to create anything your mind can imagine, using only a few basic materials, tools you already have at home, and simple techniques!

Sketching

Before starting any new project, the first thing I do is reach for a pencil and paper to do a basic sketch. This not only helps me envision what my finished craft may look like, it also allows me to think about the materials I might use and the project's basic construction. Keep in mind that this design doodle is not the finished product and doesn't have to be a work of art. It's simply a roadmap to your destination!

MATERIALS

Making magic for the holidays and every day doesn't require carts full of craft supplies . . . only a handful of talented basic materials. Although there are no hard-and-fast rules, I've divided the materials into three categories describing the role they play in most projects:

STRUCTURE
Materials used for building the base of a project

STYLE
Materials used for defining the look of a project

SPARKLE
Materials used for giving your project that extra finishing touch

STRUCTURE

Paperclay

One of the most important materials on your craft table is some sort of sculpting clay. This allows you to create your own original elements for a project, such as heads, hands, and so on, instead of buying premade pieces. Mixing sculpted clay elements with other kinds of materials, such as paper and glitter, will give your work a truly one-of-a-kind look.

After trying almost every sculpting material on the market, ranging from polymer clays that require oven baking, to messy and hard-to-mix instant papier-mâché, I have found what I consider to be the ultimate clay for crafting. It's called Paperclay. Its texture is like a paper pulp; it's easily sculpted, holds fine detail, and air-dries to an ultra-hard, sandable finish. It's inexpensive and can be purchased at most craft stores, or ordered wholesale direct from the company in large or small amounts. Paperclay is used in many of my projects, but you can use any sculptable clay material instead.

Styrofoam

Nothing makes creating a lightweight form for sculpting upon better than Styrofoam. It's found in basic shapes, from various sizes of balls to sheets and cones. It can be cut with a serrated kitchen knife, and pieces can be combined and attached together to make practically any shape imaginable.

It's very important to remember when building a structure from Styrofoam that glue is not very helpful in holding it together. White glue is too slow to stick and has little effect on the porous material, and hot glue melts the Styrofoam completely. The best technique for joining pieces of Styrofoam together and making the structure much stronger is with round toothpicks.

Styrofoam usually comes in standard white and green. I prefer the white for aesthetic reasons, but there is absolutely no difference between the makeup of the two. Do not confuse green Styrofoam with a floral foam called Oasis; this is a completely different material and will not work for our projects.

Packing Styrofoam can also be recycled for crafting, but tends to have a slick surface that's not as friendly to cutting and shaping. I save every scrap of Styrofoam, large or small, just in case it's needed for a future project.

Cardboard

There are many different weights and varieties of cardboard available at art supply stores as well as all around the house.

Poster board is a really lightweight cardboard that has a slick, clean surface, rolls easily, and is the perfect material for making cones for party hats.

Chipboard is made from recycled and compressed paper and comes in many different thicknesses. It's available in large and small sheets at art or craft supply stores. Its advantages over other cardboards are usually its weight and the ability to bond to itself very quickly with white glue. It paints without warping or wrinkling and is durable enough to be sanded on the edges to soften its rigidness.

Found boards are types of cardboard that are found and recycled from around the home. Many of my projects require cardboard tubes, and while I would like to pretend that I go to the cardboard tube store for those, in reality I usually go to the kitchen and try to free the tube from the still-full roll of paper towels. You can also use rolls from toilet tissue and wrapping paper. So to avoid the frenzy of leaving your paper products in a heap, save empty tubes from any available source.

Other found boards include packing cardboards and the backs of containers, such as your morning cereal box.

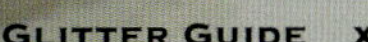

Card Stock

Many crafts require small bits of paper to be used for details such as ears or banners. Instead of using scrapbook papers that I may or may not have on my craft table, I use plain white 110-pound card stock and paint it with acrylics to get the color I need. Another benefit of this process is that the paper add-ons will match the painted sculpted body exactly. Card stock is inexpensive, completely versatile for sketching or crafting, and available in large packages alongside standard copy paper.

Glue

While adhesives are considered by some to be a sticky subject, for me it's pretty straightforward. Sometimes the more basic a material is, the better it is, and I have found this to be true with glue! Almost anything I make can be stuck together with either white glue or hot glue.

White glue is good for adhering paper, holding glitter in place, and any task not requiring instant stick. If you change your mind within a few minutes about where something is placed, it's likely you can pull it apart and reposition it.

Hot glue is great for instant glueification. It will hold the seam of a cardboard cone firmly shut, stick the fur of a marabou strand to a glittered surface, and perform many other tasks quickly. Its downsides are that it's immediately permanent, which can be a good or bad thing; it completely wrecks the surface of the item it's glued to; it's often messy, with lots of unsightly strings; and it has the ability to give you blisters if you get it on your fingers—which I have done, oh so many times!

Many projects require a combination of white and hot glues, so keep both on your table and you will not get stuck!

Gesso

Gesso is useful to have but not absolutely necessary. It's best known for being used as the primer for stretched artists' canvas. Gesso resembles white paint but has the thickness and some of the properties of a wet Plaster of Paris. It can be applied with a brush in different directions onto a surface needing texture, or used as filler on a surface you want to be smooth and free of cracks.

Once it's dry, gesso has a sandable surface and accepts paint easily. One large container will last most crafters a really long time. Its price ranges from inexpensive to pricey, depending on the brand. For general crafting, I go with the less expensive.

Wire

When you need a piece of wire, nothing else will do! There are many sizes and types of this bendable material available, but for my projects I use floral wire, which is inexpensive and available at craft stores.

It comes packaged perfectly straight and is precut to a standard 18-inch length. Its thickness is listed by gauge. The smaller the number, the thicker the wire; the higher the number, the thinner the wire—which can be a confusing system to creative people like myself.

I tend to use only a few gauges:

- 16-gauge is the strongest and perfect for making such things as arms and legs.
- 18-gauge is sturdy but flexible enough to be bent into freeform shapes.
- 20-gauge to 32-gauge are very thin wires that are great for holding small paper banners or other small details.

When a project calls for a length of painted wire, it refers to wire that has been wrapped with floral tape and painted for that specific project (see "How to Paint and Stripe a Wire," page xxi).

Floral Tape

What looks like a flimsy roll of paper tape with limited stickiness is actually one of the most valuable supplies on my craft table. I use it to wrap lengths of wire to soften the harshness of the metal and prepare the surface for painting and striping. Without floral tape, it's almost impossible to get paint to stick permanently, and the uncoated wire will eventually rust onto the rest of your project.

The trick to using floral tape is understanding that its glue is released only when the tape is pulled.

Dowels, Skewers, and Toothpicks

No craft table should be without this band of wooden wonders. They can be used as materials as well as tools. The simple ¼-inch wooden dowel like those sold in the bakery section of the craft store, for supporting wedding cakes, is the start of many projects, including the body of my folk art figures, such as Candy Claus (page 101).

Skewers, sold in the kitchen department for making kebabs, are useful as tools, and cupcake picks are useful for their original intended purpose.

The last in this trio is the toothpick, available in round and flat. I prefer round. These little helpful splinters are always there when you need them, from bringing Styrofoam pieces closer together, to serving as small flagpoles, to holding painted things to dry. If you have not yet discovered the joy of toothpicks, just set some on your craft table and you will quickly see everything there is to do with them.

Wooden Balls

Every craft store has an unfinished wood section with hundreds of little wooden doodads for crafting. Within that area are bags of small wooden balls ranging in size from less than ½ inch to several inches in diameter. They make perfect little heads for projects such as the Glitter Pixies (page 83) or the Pinecone Gnome (page 1).

Boxes

In the past few years, papier-mâché boxes and buckets have become very popular with crafters. They are an unassuming brown paper box on store shelves, but in the hands of a crafter they're quickly transformed into glittered goodness. Sculpted heads and toppers can easily be attached to them, using glue or wire.

STYLE

Paint

Almost every project I do requires acrylic paints for base coating or adding final details. Acrylic paint is water-based and dries quickly. There are many different kinds to choose from, with prices ranging from less than $1 to almost $20 per color. Price differences vary with the quality of the pigments used to make them, the brand, and whether they are bottled liquid or packaged in tubes.

While I know you get what you pay for, I still prefer the bottles of liquid acrylics commonly found in craft supply stores for less than $1 each. They have a rich matte color that blends and covers pretty well. As with acrylics of any cost, some colors such as orange, hot pink, and red require multiple coats before they start to look even.

Chenille Stems

These little fuzzy wires, often referred to as pipe cleaners, are one of my favorite crafting materials. They are easily cut with scissors and available in every color of the rainbow. The standard chenille stems with the ends bent over are good for making such things as arms and legs, while bump chenille stems and fuzzy chenille stems make fuzzier things such as beards, hair, or animals much more realistic. Small chenille stems are useful for adding finer details and accessories such as a bow tie, ears, or a tail.

Flocking Powder

Flocking powder has been around forever but has only become easily available at craft stores in the last few years. Made up of small fibers, it's great for adding to anything needing a texture like beards or animal fur or for giving dimension to patterns and stripes. To apply, it's best to brush the surface with a layer of white glue and gently crumble the flocking material between your fingers to distribute it evenly. Keep in mind that flocking takes practice and is not ideal for children.

Crepe Paper

Many people think that crepe paper sold on the roll can only be used as birthday party streamers. However, sewing and gathering multiple layers of it together transforms it into Paper Festooning, a multifaceted material for creating holiday favors and an endless array of decorative trims. The process of making festooning is shown on page xxiii, and it is used in many of the crafts throughout this book.

Marabou

If you're planning to make a party hat, you will definitely need marabou. These feathers sewn onto cotton cording, sold as boas in the craft department, can be cut to the length needed and hot glued onto any project needing a little fluff!

Felt and Fabrics

Sometimes the addition of a soft material is needed for creating things such as clothing. The use of any material resembling fabric scares many crafters who lack the ability to sew, but for those who are challenged with a needle, the ideal material is felt.

The advantage of using felt over traditional fabric is that its cut edges do not fray and require no hemming. I love it not only for its ease of use but also for its bold colors and sculptural qualities.

Another user-friendly fabric is flannel. Generally used for such things as pajamas, it has a very soft nap, which camouflages two seams when glued together on tiny shirts and pants.

SPARKLE

GLITTER

The best way to add sparkle to your project is with a sprinkling of glitter. When I first started crafting, there were not many glitter options, but today's market offers a multitude of sizes and colors.

Here are the three I use most often:

- Ultrafine glitter is perfect for almost any project. Ultrafine describes the size of its tiny crystals. This glitter is very twinkly, and somewhat translucent, which allows the color underneath it to show through. If you would like to use a particular paint color but can't find a matching glitter, just use an ultrafine crystalline (no color) over the paint for a perfect match, plus sparkle.
- Elementary school or chunky-style glitter is what I consider to be the most common of all glitters. It's very coarse and opaque, and it comes in a limited color palette. It's great for creating bold patterns and adding texture, but is almost impossible to use on fine details such as faces or stripes.
- Crushed glass glitter is certainly the most glamorous of the group of glitters. It is often referred to as German glass glitter because of its early use in handmade items imported from Europe. Glass glitter will give your projects a vintage quality unobtainable in almost any other way. The color coating on the glass contains real silver, which tarnishes over time, giving your project an authentic timeworn look. This is important to know, so it's not used on projects where an aged look is not desired. What's beautiful silver today could be black as coal tomorrow. The tarnishing effect can be delayed by keeping it under glass, since contact with air is what makes it turn black.

GOLD LEAF

Nothing looks more reflective or like real gold when applied to decorative items than a material called Gold Leaf. It is readily available where craft supplies are sold and comes packaged in very thin sheets. Depending on the type you buy, the material may or may not contain real gold, but either way it will look like it! The application can be tricky but requires more patience than actual skill. You must start by brushing a gold leaf adhesive (purchased with gold leaf) over the areas you would like to have gold leaf. Let the adhesive dry until tacky, and place a sheet of leaf over the area and rub with your finger or a soft brush. This will transfer the gold from the sheet to the tackiness of the adhesive.

TOOLS

Craft stores are full of specialty tools designed for crafting, with each one performing a specific or single task. While it's fun to have these gadgets, which in some cases work great, buying them is expensive and you practically need a toolshed in which to keep them all.

Here's a list of simple tools found on my craft table and used daily.

CUTTING TOOLS

Scissors

I should start by saying that you should always have two pairs of scissors, one for general crafting and another for cutting fabrics only, but I know that it's hard to always abide by this rule, and the scissors I use to cut fabric with often end up cutting wire and cardboard. I like a nice sharp pair of metal scissors that can be resharpened when needed, but for the projects in this book, any scissors that cut will work just fine.

Pinking Shears

There are lots of different craft scissors that can be used to give a decorative edge to paper, fabrics, or felt. However, I prefer a standard pair of pinking shears that are commonly found in the sewing department.

Craft Knife

Many people know this as an X-ACTO knife, referring to the leading name brand. It's basically a small knife with a blade that can be changed once it becomes dull.

Wire Cutters

A good pair of wire cutters is one of the most necessary tools needed for crafting. I want them to be industrial enough to cut through wires of different thicknesses, so I prefer the wire cutters found at the hardware store over those found in craft stores.

Easy Cutting Tool

This is by far the most exotic hand tool I own. It looks like a pair of pliers, but is actually used for cutting wooden dowels and skewers cleanly at any angle, without splintering the end. They are inexpensive and seem to hide in the model-building section of the craft store. Don't sweat it if you don't have one. I didn't have one for years! Just use a small hacksaw instead.

Serrated Kitchen Knife

One of the most useful tools on your craft table comes from your dinner table. A basic serrated knife used for cutting bread or steak is perfect for cutting things that require a longer blade than the one found in a craft knife. This is my favorite tool for cutting Styrofoam.

OTHER TOOLS

Needle-Nose Pliers
The benefit of these pointy pliers is their ability to curl the ends of wire around their rounded point. I buy these at the hardware store as well. They are also sold as jewelry pliers in craft stores.

Clay-Sculpting Tool
Although many commercial sculpting tools are available for working with clay, I find that household items such as toothpicks, skewers, and plastic forks often work just as well as a "real" tool.

Drill
Many projects require you to drill a hole for attaching accessories and so forth. I use a standard household drill from the hardware store, equipped with a set of drill bits ranging from small to large.

Punches
The task of cutting out dozens of small shapes from paper is done effortlessly with the aid of hand punches. Punches can be used in two very different ways. You can use them for cutting out shapes needed as a material, or as a tool for leaving a shaped opening in your paper, and sometimes both. Although they are available in practically every shape, I use a standard hole punch for making small uniform holes, and various circle punches. I also use a small star punch for making a tree topper for a Tiny Tannenbaum (see page 9).

Paintbrushes
Most of my projects require a small detail brush for the face, a medium-sized round bristle brush, and slightly flat brushes of varying widths for painting larger areas. I prefer synthetic nylon bristles for craft work because of their sturdiness. Natural bristle brushes tend to shed and leave bristles in your paint.

Sewing Tools
Having a sewing machine on your craft table is great, but any projects in this book requiring stitching can just as easily be done by hand . . . and you will never run out of bobbin. If you do have a machine and plan to use it for creating paper festooning (page xxiii), you should

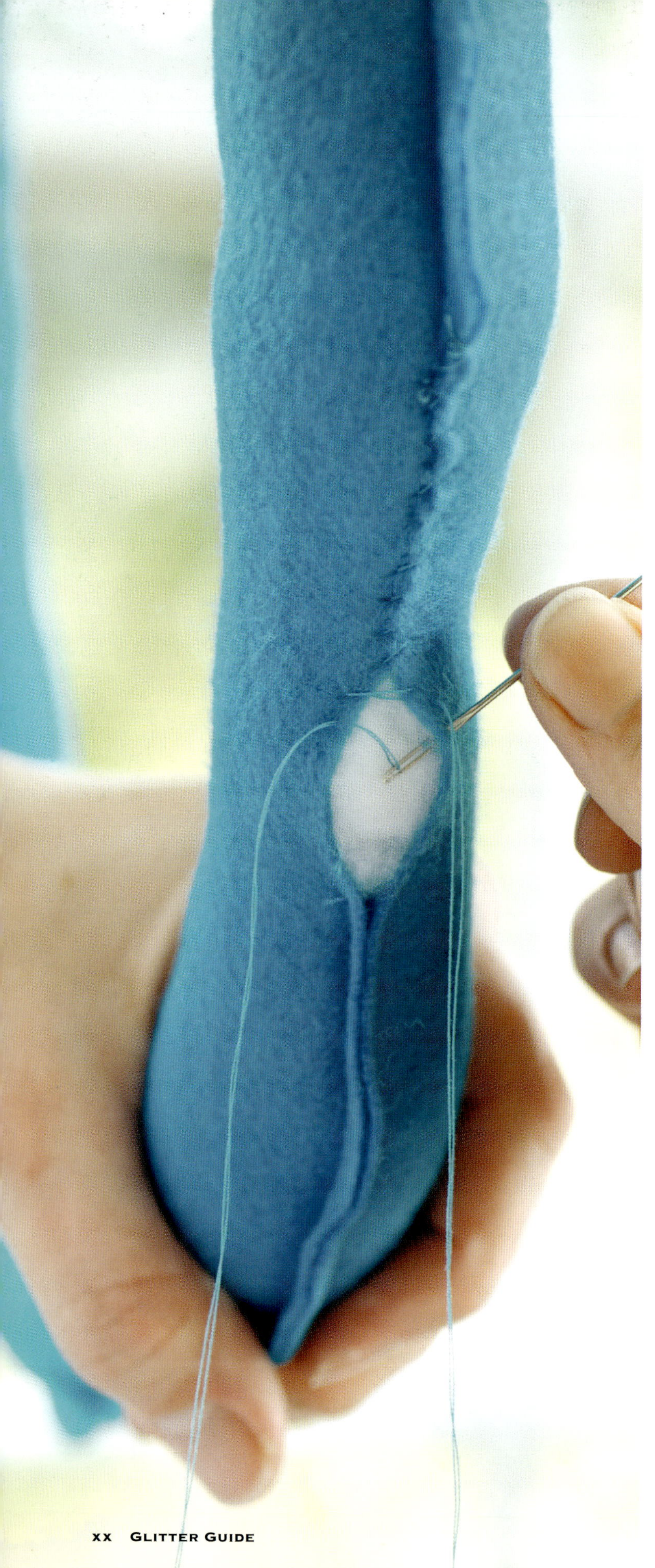

outfit it with a pleating foot to make it go super fast. If hand-sewing, all that will be needed is a standard pack of hand sewing needles in sizes you're comfortable using.

Quilling Tool

Although I rarely use this tool (usually because I can't locate it), it can be a life saver on a craft that calls for lots of small strips of paper to be curled tightly. My replacement for the quilling tool is simply a toothpick, which in most cases works fine, but the actual tool designed for quilling or curling paper does have some advantages. The tip end of a quilling tool has a short piece of metal with a split down the middle. This split holds the end of your paper strip, allowing it to roll up much tighter than an unsecured end wrapped onto a toothpick. Quilling tools are inexpensive and readily available at most craft stores.

In addition to the aforementioned tools, every craft table should have the following basic necessities:

- Stapler
- Ruler
- Dressmaker's measuring tape
- Standard #2 and colored pencils
- Pencil sharpener

BASIC TECHNIQUES

In addition to having basic materials and tools, it's good to develop a few basic techniques that you can rely on when starting a new project. Here are a few how-tos for skills and processes used multiple times throughout this book.

How to Make a 9-inch Cone

The size of your cone is determined by the size of the circle you start with. You can make a cone any size by adjusting the diameter of the circle to be equal to twice the height of the finished cone you want. Example: If you want a cone that is 6 inches tall, you should start with a 12-inch-diameter circle.

Materials

White poster board
White glue

Tools

Pencil
Scissors
Paintbrush

1 Draw an 18-inch-diameter circle on a piece of poster board.
2 Use scissors to cut out the circle.
3 Fold the circle in half and crease.
4 Using scissors, cut along the crease. You will now have two half-circles that are the same size. Set one aside for another use.
5 With the straight side facing up, roll the half circle into a cone shape, keeping the bottom edge as even as possible.
6 Brush the seam edge with white glue and press together.

How to Paint and Stripe a Wire

Wires can be painted in any color combination you choose, and many of the projects in this book call for painted wires.

Materials

Floral stem wire
White floral tape
Acrylic paints

Tools

Paintbrush

1 Beginning at the top of the floral stem wire, fold the end of the floral tape around at a slight angle and hold with your fingers.
2 Twist the wire in your fingers as you gently pull the floral tape in a downward motion to cover the wire as it turns. The edges of the floral tape should overlap only slightly. Be careful not to pull too hard or the floral tape will tear.
3 Work your way to the bottom of the wire, pinch the tape at the end of the wire, and tear the floral tape.
4 Paint the covered wire with a base coat of white acrylic paint and allow to dry.
5 Using a small paintbrush, add stripes to the wire.

How to Apply Glitter

MATERIALS
White glue
Glitter

TOOLS
Paintbrush

1 Brush a small section of your surface evenly with white glue.
2 Sprinkle glitter over the glue area. With your hand, gently press the glitter into the glue. Allow any excess glitter to fall away.
3 Continue brushing with white glue, sprinkling with glitter, and pressing in, until the entire cone is covered. Allow the glue to dry completely.

Working with Paperclay

MATERIALS
Paperclay
Small bowl of water

TOOLS
Sealable plastic bag
Damp paper towel (optional)
220-grit sandpaper

1 After opening a package of Paperclay, it's important to put what is not being used immediately in a sealable plastic bag. This will keep the clay moist and easy to work with. If the clay becomes too soft, remove it from the bag for a short time; if it becomes too hard, put it back into the plastic bag along with a damp paper towel.
2 The biggest trick to working with Paperclay is dipping your fingers into a small bowl of water throughout the sculpting process for smoothing the clay. Sometimes an area you're sculpting will become sticky if dampened too much. If this happens, just give it a couple of minutes to dry and it will be ready to continue.
3 When your finished sculpture has had time to dry and harden, use a 220-grit sandpaper to lightly buff its surface until smooth.

How to Paint a Face

MATERIALS
Acrylic paint

TOOLS
Paintbrushes

1 Although each face is uniquely different, I generally start by painting the entire face with the base color I want the face to be.
2 Next I use a process that I call color blocking, which simply means to paint areas such as the eyes and mouth with a solid color.
3 Then, with a fine brush, continue with shading and adding the final details, such as the pupils and eyelashes, teeth, and other characteristics, such as warts, and so on.

How to Make Paper Festooning

Materials

Rolls of crepe paper
Coordinating thread

Tools

Pinking shears
Scissors
Straight pins
Sewing needle
Sewing machine with a pleating foot (optional)

1. Begin by layering four long pieces of crepe paper. Use two different colors and alternate. Sewing will shorten the length of your original crepe paper strips, so determine how much you need and double that length before sewing.
2. Straighten out all the layers, then trim all the pieces to the same length with pinking shears or scissors and pin together at one end. You should have four pieces of crepe paper that are the same length, pinned together at one end. Now you're ready to start sewing.
3. At the end with the straight pin, tie the thread tail around the pin to anchor it.
4. Start by straight stitching down the center of the crepe paper, pulling the thread to gather the paper toward the end with the secured straight pin, while pulling the thread at the other end.
5. Continue to stitch and gather the entire length of paper slowly and carefully so that you don't tear the paper.
6. When you have gathered the paper evenly and have a piece of festooning the length desired, make a small fold, then stitch to secure the end and tie off the thread.
7. Finish by gently separating the layers and fanning them out with your fingers. Sometimes the crepe paper sticks together within the folds, which makes it hard to separate. If this happens, try separating it with a straight pin or toothpick.
8. If you have a sewing machine and a pleating foot, you can quickly make whole rolls of festooning. Layer up your crepe paper as described for hand sewing and set your machine to the longest stitch setting. Match the bobbin to the bottom paper color and the top thread to the top paper color. Sew down the center. The pleating foot will gather the paper as you sew.

Pinecone Gnome

At holiday time, there's no place like home.
This is true for all, even glitter gnomes.
The twenty-fourth is the start of their celebration,
the official groundbreaking for their anticipation!

Everyone in town is given a sack,
with straps to hold it on their back,
then they are off to mushroom pick,
like a little band of Old Saint Nicks!

When all the fungi are finally found,
they bring their bounty back to town.
In colors blue, pink, red, and green,
it's a holiday rainbow of mushroom trees!

At the spectrum's end is something better than gold,
that can't be purchased and can't be sold.
It is Christmas day in the land of Gnome,
bringing celebration to every home!

Pinecone Glitter Gnome

It amazes me that elf-like creatures live virtually all around us but manage for the most part to have very little interaction with humans. I occasionally see them collecting honey (I assume for baking) from a swarm of ambitious bees that sell their nectars underneath my boxwood hedge, but on most days, proof of their existence is represented by only a random footprint here and there. If sightings of gnomes are rare at your home, worry not, and just make your own!

1 Make the body. Brush the entire pinecone with a coat of gesso or white acrylic paint. Allow to dry.

2 Create a gradient color effect on the pinecone by painting the top half light blue and the bottom half light green. While the two colors are still wet, use a paintbrush to blend them together toward the center.

3

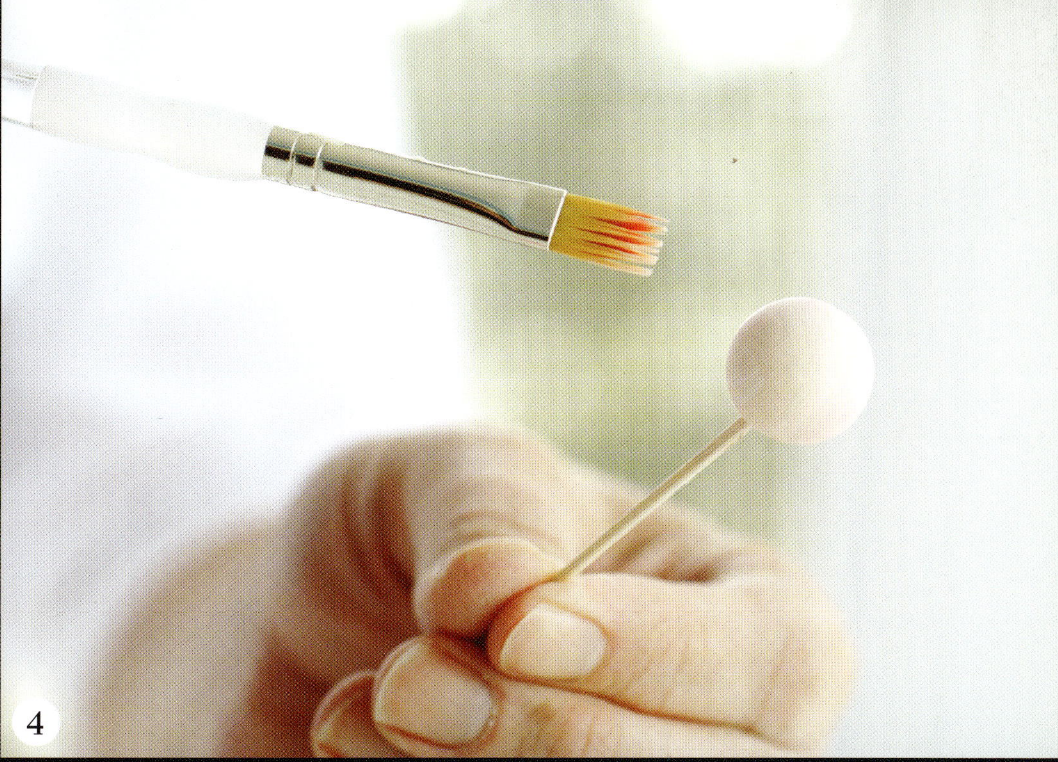

4

3 Make the head. Drill a hole approximately ¼ inch deep into the wooden craft ball using a 1/16-inch bit.

4 To hold the wooden ball for painting, place it on a toothpick. Coat it with flesh-colored acrylic paint. Dry brush pink onto the cheeks. Allow to dry.

5 Use a small detail brush and white acrylic paint to color block the eyebrows, eyes, and mustache.

6 Use a small brush to add the details of the eyes and mouth. Allow to dry. For the nose, use white glue to attach a small ball of Paperclay. Use a hairdryer to harden the Paperclay; paint the nose pink, and allow it to dry. You could use a bead for the nose, if you prefer.

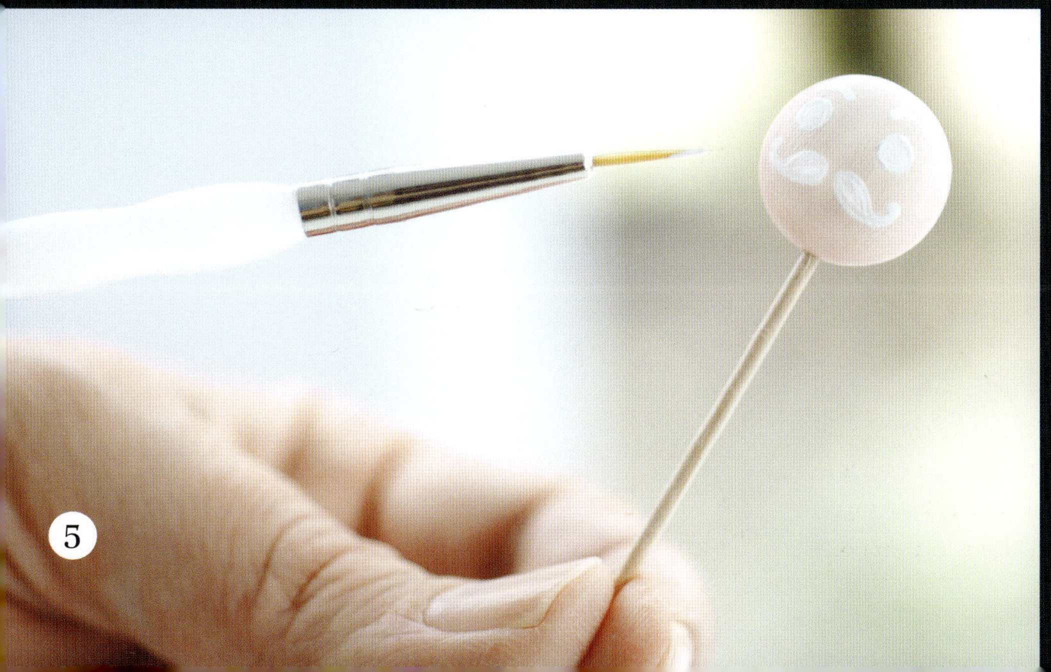

5

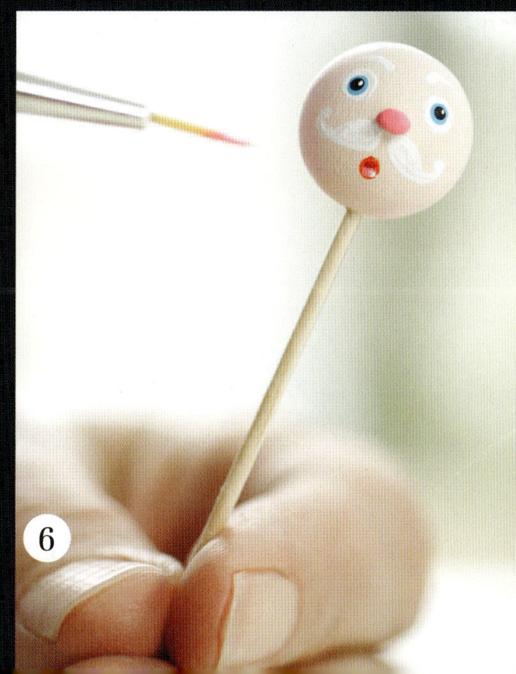

6

7
8
9
10
11
12

7 Use wire cutters to cut a 2-inch piece of light blue regular chenille stem and coil it around a kitchen skewer to shape it. Use hot glue to attach one end of the chenille to the top of the pinecone. Gently pull the other end up to create the neck.

8 Place a small amount of white glue on the end of the chenille stem neck and place the head on it.

9 Brush the pinecone with white glue and sprinkle with glitter.

10 Make the beard. Use wire cutters to cut one section from the white bump chenille stem. Bend the ends around the head to the back to create the hair. Trim any excess and secure with hot glue.

11 To cover the back of the head, fold both ends of another section of white bump chenille stem toward the center to form a bean shape, as shown. Attach it with hot glue.

12 Make the arms. Use wire cutters to cut one 7½-inch piece of light blue regular chenille stem. Use a ruler to find the middle of the stem and fold both ends to the center, as shown.

13 Make the mittens. Use wire cutters to cut two 1-inch pieces of red regular chenille stem and wrap around the ends of the blue chenille arms. Use hot glue to attach the arms to the back of the gnome, just below the white chenille hair.

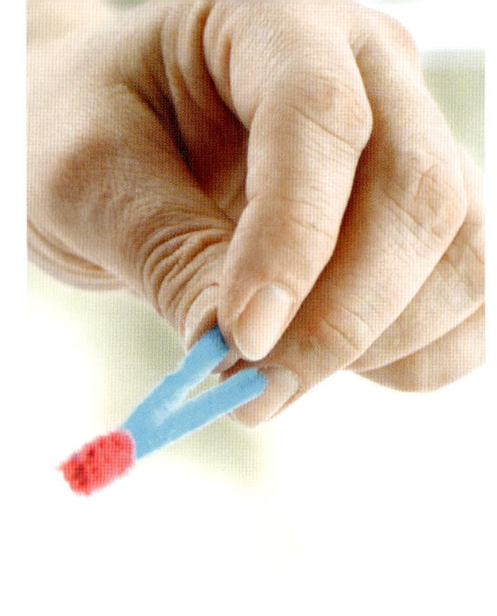

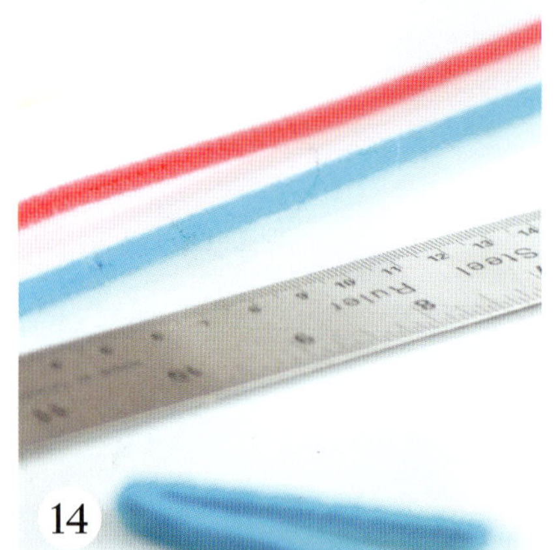

14 Make the legs. Cut two 4½-inch pieces of medium blue regular chenille stem and two 1½-inch pieces of hot pink regular chenille stem. Fold both of the blue pieces in half and wrap one of the pink pieces around the bent end of each leg to create shoes.

15 Bend a slight curve into each of the legs and twist the tops. Insert the legs between the petals of the pinecone to find a good fit and trim the chenille stems to length. Every pinecone is different, but my gnome's legs measure approximately ¾ inch, when standing.

16 Make the base. Use scissors to cut a 1½-inch-diameter circle from lightweight cardboard. Coat both sides with gesso or white acrylic paint and allow it to dry. Use hot glue to attach the feet of the gnome to the center of the base. Brush the base with white glue and sprinkle it with glitter.

17 Make small mushrooms from Paperclay. Push them onto toothpicks and allow the Paperclay to harden. Paint the mushrooms, as shown, and set them aside to dry. If you don't want to sculpt with Paperclay, you could substitute small found objects or beads for the mushrooms. Use a star punch to make yellow card stock stars and attach them to the tops of the mushrooms with white glue.

18

20

19

18 Make the backpack. Copy the gnome backpack pattern pieces on card stock and use scissors to cut them out. Use a pencil to trace the pattern onto lightweight cardboard and cut out with scissors. Give the backpack pieces a slight curve by gently shaping them around a wooden dowel. Attach the bottom curves of the two pieces together using white glue and hold together until dry. This will close the bottom opening and add support. Coat the entire backpack with gesso or white acrylic paint and allow it to dry. Brush with white glue and sprinkle it with glitter. Use hot glue to attach the backpack to the gnome. Use wire cutters to trim one of the mushroom toothpicks and use hot glue to secure it in the gnome's hand.

19 Use wire cutters to trim the remaining mushroom toothpicks and drop them into the gnome's backpack.

20 Make the hat. Copy the Gnome Hat Pattern on card stock. Use scissors to cut it out. Roll it into a cone and secure the seam with hot glue. Paint and add polka dots to the hat, and allow it to dry. Use hot glue to attach the hat to the top of the gnome's head. Now make more, so your gnome has friends!

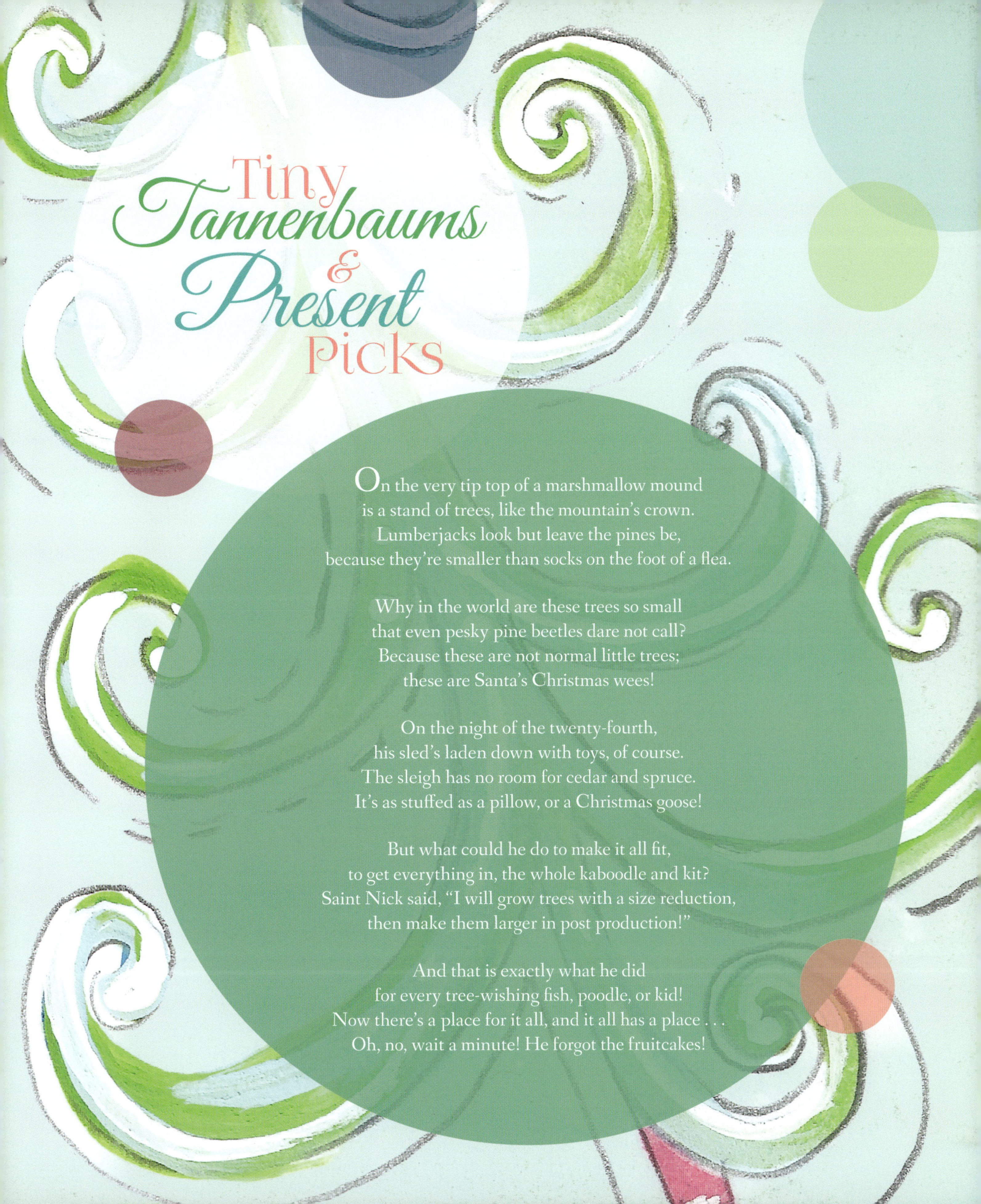

Tiny Tannenbaums & Present Picks

On the very tip top of a marshmallow mound
is a stand of trees, like the mountain's crown.
Lumberjacks look but leave the pines be,
because they're smaller than socks on the foot of a flea.

Why in the world are these trees so small
that even pesky pine beetles dare not call?
Because these are not normal little trees;
these are Santa's Christmas wees!

On the night of the twenty-fourth,
his sled's laden down with toys, of course.
The sleigh has no room for cedar and spruce.
It's as stuffed as a pillow, or a Christmas goose!

But what could he do to make it all fit,
to get everything in, the whole kaboodle and kit?
Saint Nick said, "I will grow trees with a size reduction,
then make them larger in post production!"

And that is exactly what he did
for every tree-wishing fish, poodle, or kid!
Now there's a place for it all, and it all has a place . . .
Oh, no, wait a minute! He forgot the fruitcakes!

1

2

HERE'S EVERYTHING NEEDED FOR THIS MAKE AND DO! GATHER YOUR GLITTER, SCISSORS, AND GLUE.

Materials

Green card stock
Toothpicks
Acrylic paints
White glue
Yellow card stock
⅜-inch wooden craft blocks
Card stock in assorted colors, for the present bows

Tools

Craft knife
Ruler
Self-healing mat
Scissors
Paintbrushes
Styrofoam
Quilling tool or toothpick
¼-inch star punch
Drill with 1⁄16-inch bit

Tiny Tannenbaums and Present Picks

I will never forget being completely mesmerized by a tray of tree-topped cupcakes delivered to my classroom Christmas party when I was in second grade. Even though my mouth watered to taste what looked to be a completely yummy treat, I could not bear the thought of having only one of those beautiful little pines. So, I made a quick deal with the boy sitting behind me and handed over my cupcake for his topper. Although I'm sure that I missed out on a great sugar rush at the time, to this day I do not regret the swap! Now I can make myself an entire forest of these wee wonders, and so can you!

1 Using a craft knife, ruler, and a self-healing mat, cut a 5 × ¾-inch strip of green card stock. Cut the strip into five 1-inch pieces.

2 Fringe the edge of each piece by snipping into them approximately ⅜ inch apart with scissors, leaving approximately ⅜ inch at the top. Be careful not to go all the way through. These pieces will become the branches of your wee tree.

3 Make the tree trunk. Paint a toothpick with white acrylic paint and allow it to dry. When making lots of trees, I find it easier to stick a group of toothpicks into a small piece of Styrofoam and paint them all at once.

4 Add stripes to the lower half of the toothpick using a small detail brush. When the toothpick is completely dry, you can start putting up the tree!

5 Apply a bit of white glue to the toothpick approximately halfway up.

6 Press the top edge of one piece of fringed green card stock into the white glue and carefully begin wrapping around the toothpick.

7 Continue wrapping the entire strip and secure the end with a drop of white glue. This is the first row of branches.

8 Repeat this process with the other four strips until you have reached the top of the toothpick.

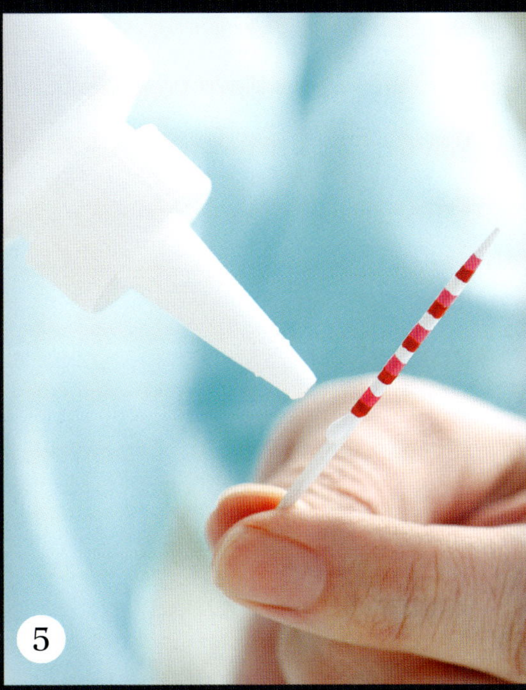

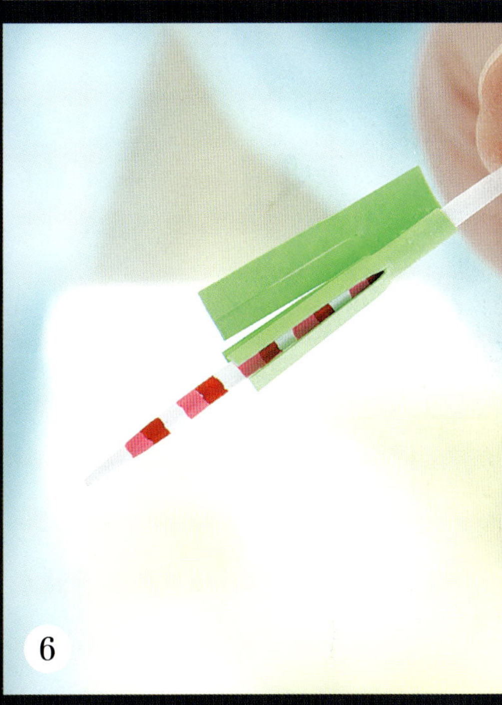

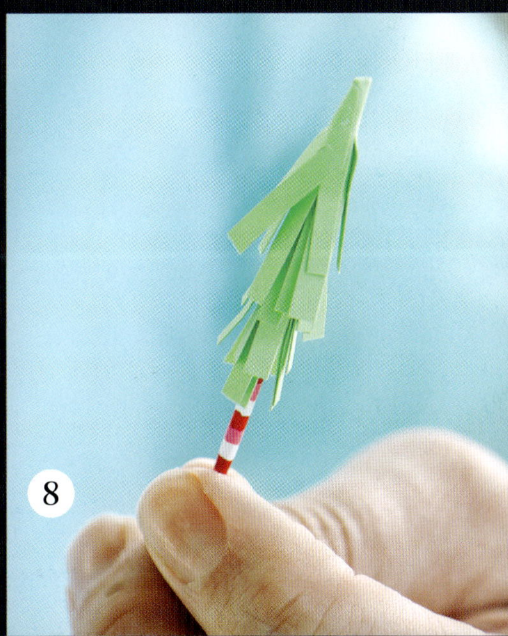

9 Once the glue is dry, use a quilling tool or another toothpick to curl each row of branches. Start at the top and work your way down. Now it's starting to look like a tree!

10 Make the topper. Make two tiny stars using a ¼-inch star punch and yellow card stock. Use white glue to attach one star to the front and one to the back of the tree top.

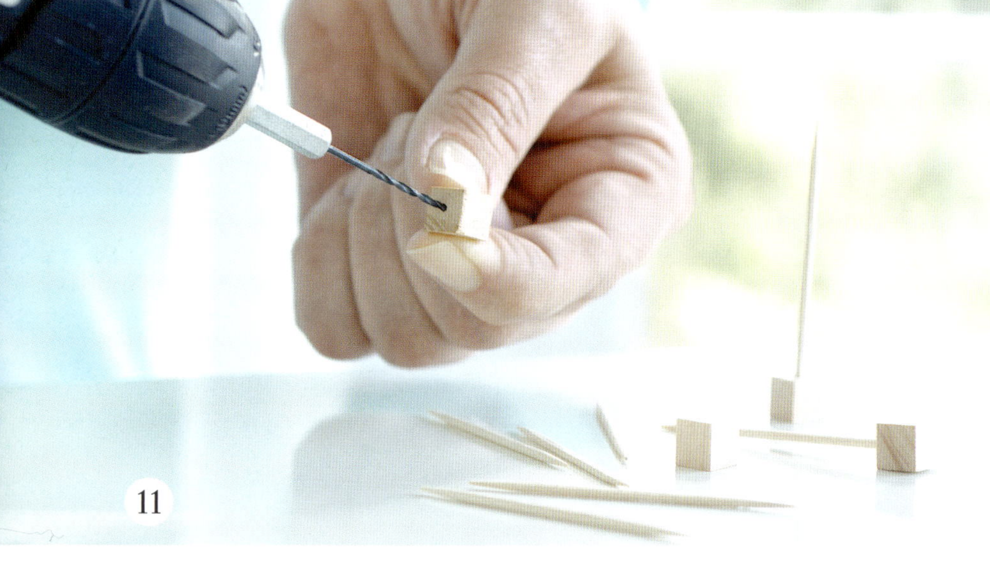

11 Make the Present Picks. Start by drilling a hole into the bottom of each ⅜-inch wooden craft block with a 1⁄16-inch drill bit. Insert a toothpick that has been dipped in white glue.

12 Base coat the wooden blocks and toothpicks with acrylic paints and allow to dry.

13 Make a small bow for each present. Use scissors to cut colored card stock into ⅛-inch × 4-inch strips. Bend the strip back and forth like an accordion, being careful not to crease the card stock. Bending it around a toothpick will help. Curl the top piece of the strip with a toothpick, as shown. Use white glue to attach the segments of the bow together.

14 Use white glue to attach the bow to the present. Add the finishing details with acrylic paint and a small brush.

15 Display your Tiny Tannenbaums and Present Picks in a bowl of marshmallows, or use them as cupcake toppers!

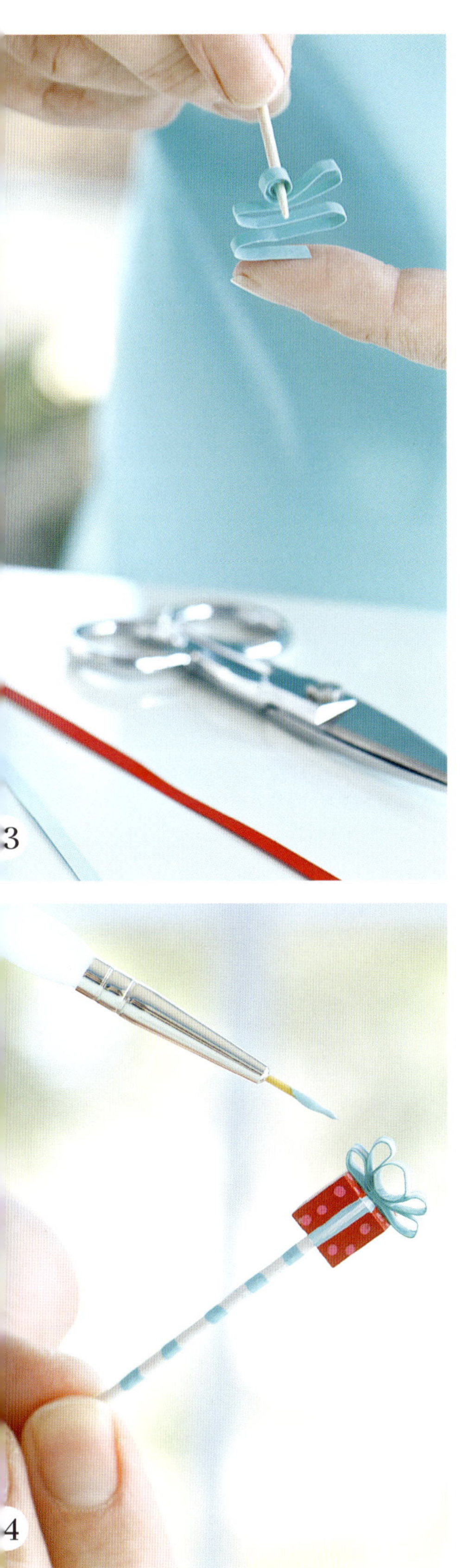
3

4

15

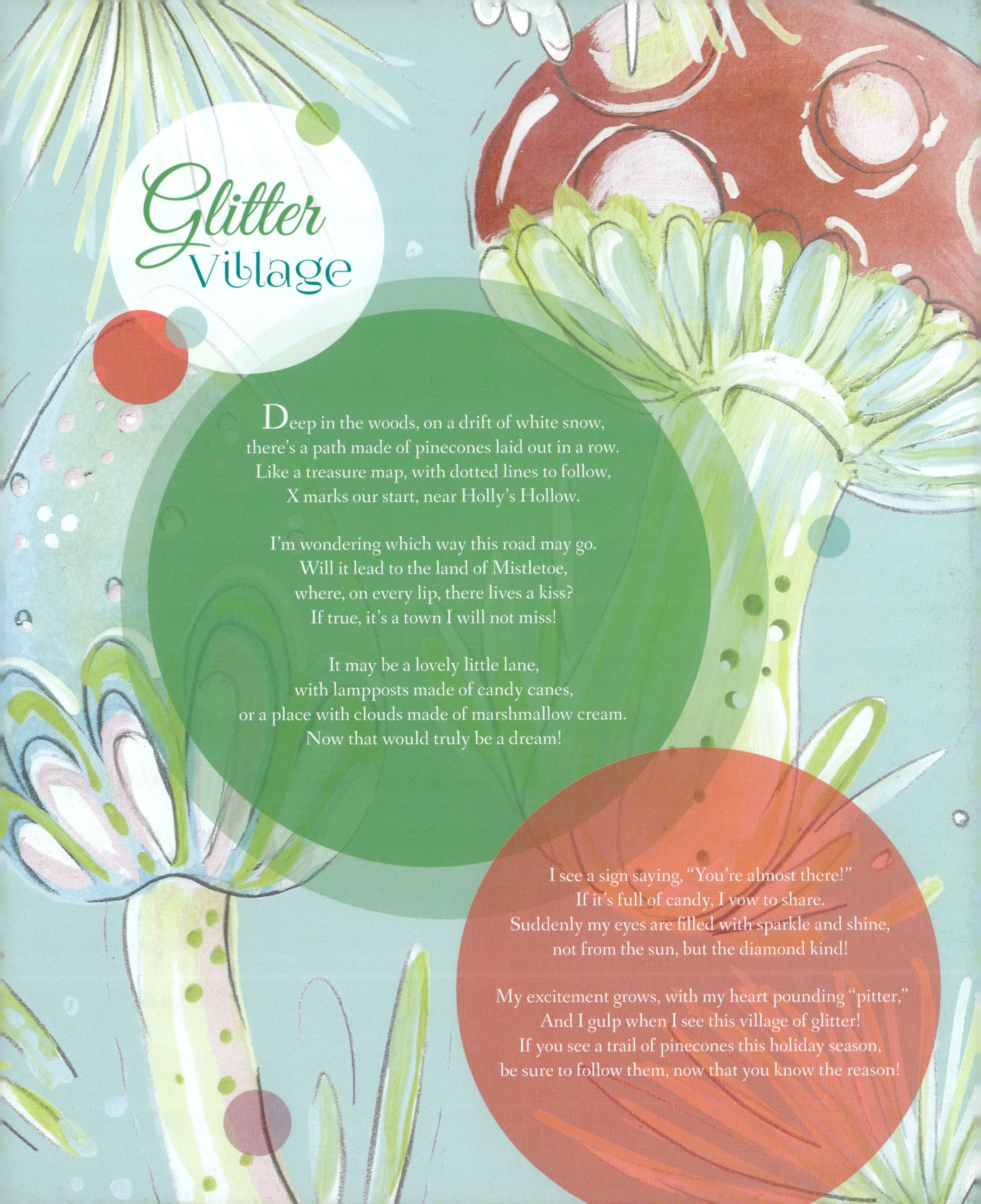

Glitter Village

Deep in the woods, on a drift of white snow,
there's a path made of pinecones laid out in a row.
Like a treasure map, with dotted lines to follow,
X marks our start, near Holly's Hollow.

I'm wondering which way this road may go.
Will it lead to the land of Mistletoe,
where, on every lip, there lives a kiss?
If true, it's a town I will not miss!

It may be a lovely little lane,
with lampposts made of candy canes,
or a place with clouds made of marshmallow cream.
Now that would truly be a dream!

I see a sign saying, "You're almost there!"
If it's full of candy, I vow to share.
Suddenly my eyes are filled with sparkle and shine,
not from the sun, but the diamond kind!

My excitement grows, with my heart pounding "pitter,"
And I gulp when I see this village of glitter!
If you see a trail of pinecones this holiday season,
be sure to follow them, now that you know the reason!

1

Here's everything needed for this make and do! Gather your glitter, scissors, and glue.

Materials

- House Pattern Pieces (page 170–173)
- Card stock
- Medium-weight cardboard
- White glue
- Brown craft paper
- Gesso
- Acrylic paint
- Gold leaf sheets
- Gold leaf adhesive
- Translucent paper or tissue paper
- Small pieces of balsa wood
- Small sisal craft trees

Tools

- Photocopier
- Scissors
- Pencil
- Craft knife
- Extra craft knife blades
- Ruler
- ½-inch-diameter dowel
- Clothespins
- Painters tape
- Paintbrushes

Glitter Village

I feel like a Christmas contractor when I'm making these miniature cardboard structures covered in paint and glitter, inspired by vintage examples called Putz (Christmas Village) houses. This little house has all the bells and whistles, from window boxes to a chimney that's crooked as a snake, and although these details take time, they are what makes this project so much fun. So put on your hard hat and start building!

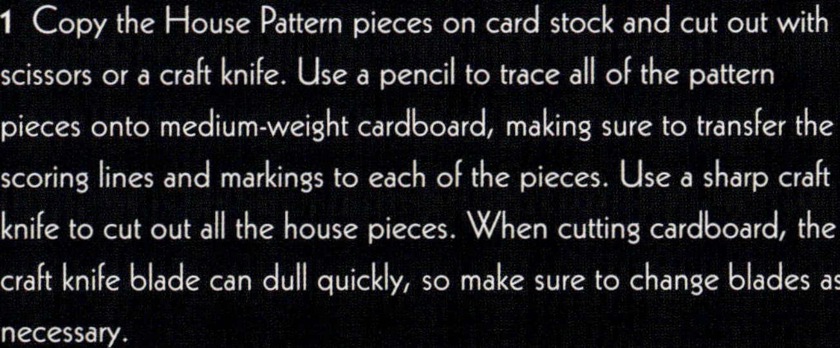

1 Copy the House Pattern pieces on card stock and cut out with scissors or a craft knife. Use a pencil to trace all of the pattern pieces onto medium-weight cardboard, making sure to transfer the scoring lines and markings to each of the pieces. Use a sharp craft knife to cut out all the house pieces. When cutting cardboard, the craft knife blade can dull quickly, so make sure to change blades as necessary.

2 Score and fold the two main house sections. Cut and score inside corner brace to reinforce the inside of the wall joints and glue the sections together with white glue.

3 Cut tabs and attach them to the walls with white glue, as shown. This will support the roof.

4 Score and fold the roof section. Use a ½-inch-diameter dowel or the end of a craft knife to roll the cardboard gently from the center to the edge, forming a bowl shape.

5

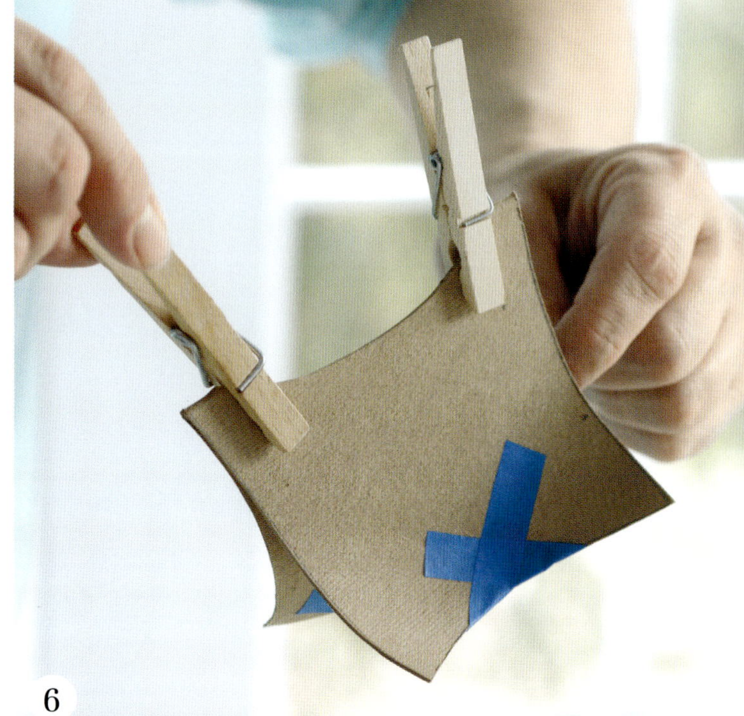
6

7

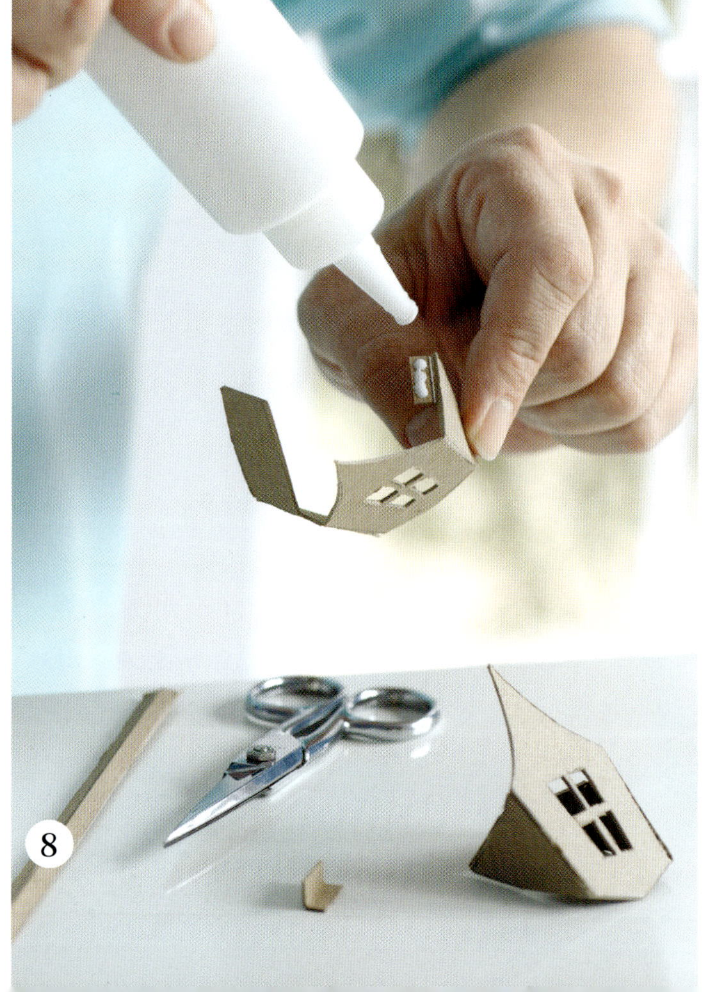
8

5 Glue and pull the edges of the slit in the lower roof edge together and reinforce from behind using a strip of brown craft paper. This forms the roof section into a bowl shape. Use painter's tape to hold the shape until the glue dries completely.

6 Glue the ridge of the roof section together using white glue. Attach clothespins to hold the ridge in place until the glue dries completely.

7 Fit the roof section to the house walls, adjusting the curves of the roof to fit the contour of the house walls. Use painter's tape to hold the roof in place until the glue dries completely. Apply glue to the four tabs you created along the upper edges of the wall sections. Attach the roof section, making sure all four sides are even.

8 Score and fold the two dormer sections and attach the end of each one with a tab to reinforce the free end.

9 Score and fold the dormer roofs and roll into shape using a ½-inch-diameter dowel or the end of a craft knife.

10 Glue the ridges of the two dormer roofs as you did the main roof. Use clothespins to hold the ridges in place until the glue dries completely.

9

10

11

12

13

14

11 When the glue on the roofs of the dormers has dried completely, fit the dormer roofs to the dormers, adjusting each roof for the best fit. Apply white glue to the top edges of the dormer sections and attach the dormer roofs to the dormers. Use painter's tape to hold the pieces in place until the glue dries completely.

12 Apply white glue to the right-hand edge of the back chimney piece and attach the outside edge of the right piece using painter's tape as a temporary support. Repeat for each of the other three joints of the chimney.

13 Score and fold the awning.

14 Glue the triangular awning support piece to the inside of the awning to help the awning hold its shape.

15 Score and fold the window boxes. Glue the two bottom edges together and allow the glue to dry completely.

16 Score the house corner trim pieces and glue them to the three corners of the house. Use trim marked House Corner Trim by Chimney for the fourth corner.

17 Use white glue to attach the window and door trim to the outside of the house and dormer sections.

18 Glue the inside edges of the window boxes and attach them to the house under the three lower windows. Attach the awning over the front door with white glue.

15

16

17

18

19 Attach the chimney to the left side of the house with white glue.

20 Brush the house and dormer walls with a coat of gesso or white acrylic paint. Allow to dry.

21 Brush all of the window mullions with gold acrylic paint. Allow to dry.

22 Brush gold leaf adhesive on the window and door mullions and apply gold leaf. [See instructions in Glitter Guide page xvii]

23 Glue small pieces of scrapbook or tissue paper to the inside backs of the door and windows.

24 Use a pencil to mark the center of the house roof and make sure the dormers fit. Trim or adjust if needed. Use white glue to attach the dormers at the center mark of the main roof. Hold the dormers in place with painter's tape until the glue dries completely.

25 Cut small pieces of balsa wood or cardboard to be used for shingles and use white glue to attach them in rows, starting from the bottom and working your way up the roof. The house will look more whimsical if the shingles are cut free-form instead of all being exactly the same.

26 Paint or stain the shingles and let dry. Apply gold leaf adhesive and gold leaf accents to the roof.

27 Color block the entire house with acrylic paint.

28 Add details with a fine paintbrush.

29 Fill the window boxes with tops cut from small sisal trees. Secure them with white glue and allow to dry.

Sparkle Forest

When I was small, a long time ago,
it was into the garden I'd often go.
I'll never forget, and always remember,
that special day in early December.

As I was picking berried holly,
a gnome appeared, short, round, and jolly.
He did not drive, I'm certain of that,
since I saw his arrival on the tail of my cat.

At first I was startled, but he quickly smiled,
"I have a present just for you, my dear child."
I said, "Christmas is still almost three weeks away,
so why am I getting a present today?"

He replied, "Under my hat is a bag full of glitter
that into the ground you should gently flitter.
Plant this sparkle, just as I say,
and a surprise you will have on Christmas day!"

So without regard for making rows,
I spread the bag like diamonds sowed.
Then I turned around, but he was gone.
That gnome, I guess, had journeyed home.

That night in bed, my mind did think,
"Would this surprise be something pink?
Or would it be nothing at all—
just a prank for which I'd fall?"

When the day came, I ran to the spot,
and disappointed I was not.
The most beautiful trees I'd ever seen,
in every color—not just green!

Now I think I understand.
My plantings grew a Glitterland!
A sparkle forest for all to see,
a field of shiny Christmas trees.

GATHER YOUR GLITTER, SCISSORS, AND GLUE. HERE'S EVERYTHING NEEDED FOR THIS MAKE AND DO!

Materials

- Water
- 1 gallon household bleach
- Sisal craft trees (available at craft stores)
- Acrylic paints
- White glue
- Glitter

Tools

- Two large glass containers
- Rubber gloves
- Paper towels
- Hairdryer (optional)
- Scissors
- Paintbrushes
- Toothbrush (optional)
- Card stock

Sparkle Forest

During the holiday season, practically every mantle, table, and shelf in my home is covered with a small forest of vintage sisal trees, or as some people call them, bottlebrush trees. And although I love the frazzled quality of my vintage ones, I really wanted some brighter ones, possibly even striped, but never found them. So, I decided to make my own by bleaching those snow-tipped dark green ones easily found everywhere during the Christmas season. But changing the color wasn't enough. I wanted stripes and a new shape, too. You will be amazed at how fun this project is, but the first few steps requiring bleach should be done by adults only.

1 Fill one glass container with clean water and a second glass container with bleach, being careful not to spill or splash it onto your clothes or surroundings. Place them side by side on a protected surface.

2 While wearing rubber gloves, hold a sisal tree by its base and submerge it in the bleach.

3 Twist and swirl the tree in the bleach until the color starts to fade. The tree will turn many shades of green, from dark to light, before turning white.

4

5

4 When the tree reaches the shade you desire, remove it from the bleach and dip it into the container of water to rinse.

5 Dip as many trees at one time as you want to have in your forest.

6 Remove the trees from the rinse water and blot them on several layers of paper towels. Discard the used bleach and rinse water. Allow the trees to dry. You can also use a hairdryer to speed up the drying process, if desired.

7 Once the trees are completely dry, you can use scissors to trim them into whimsical shapes.

8 Recolor the sisal with a base coat of white acrylic paint. Separating the bristles with an old toothbrush or your fingers before the paint dries completely will keep the paint from clumping. Allow to dry.

6

7

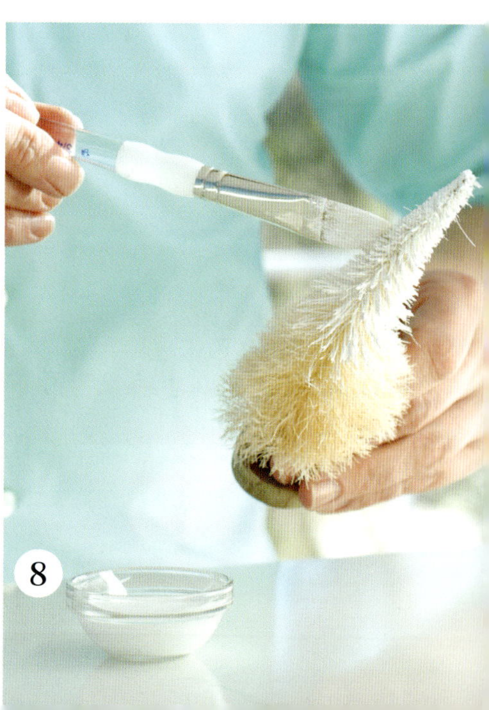
8

9 To create a striped tree, insert a folded piece of card stock into the sisal where you want the line to be. This will keep the paint from getting onto the areas that you want to leave white. Move the card stock as you turn the tree and paint all the way around. Repeat as you go up the tree. Allow to dry.

10 Paint the stem and the base with white acrylic paint and allow to dry. Add multicolored stripes and allow to dry.

11 Brush the base and sisal with white glue and sprinkle with glitter.

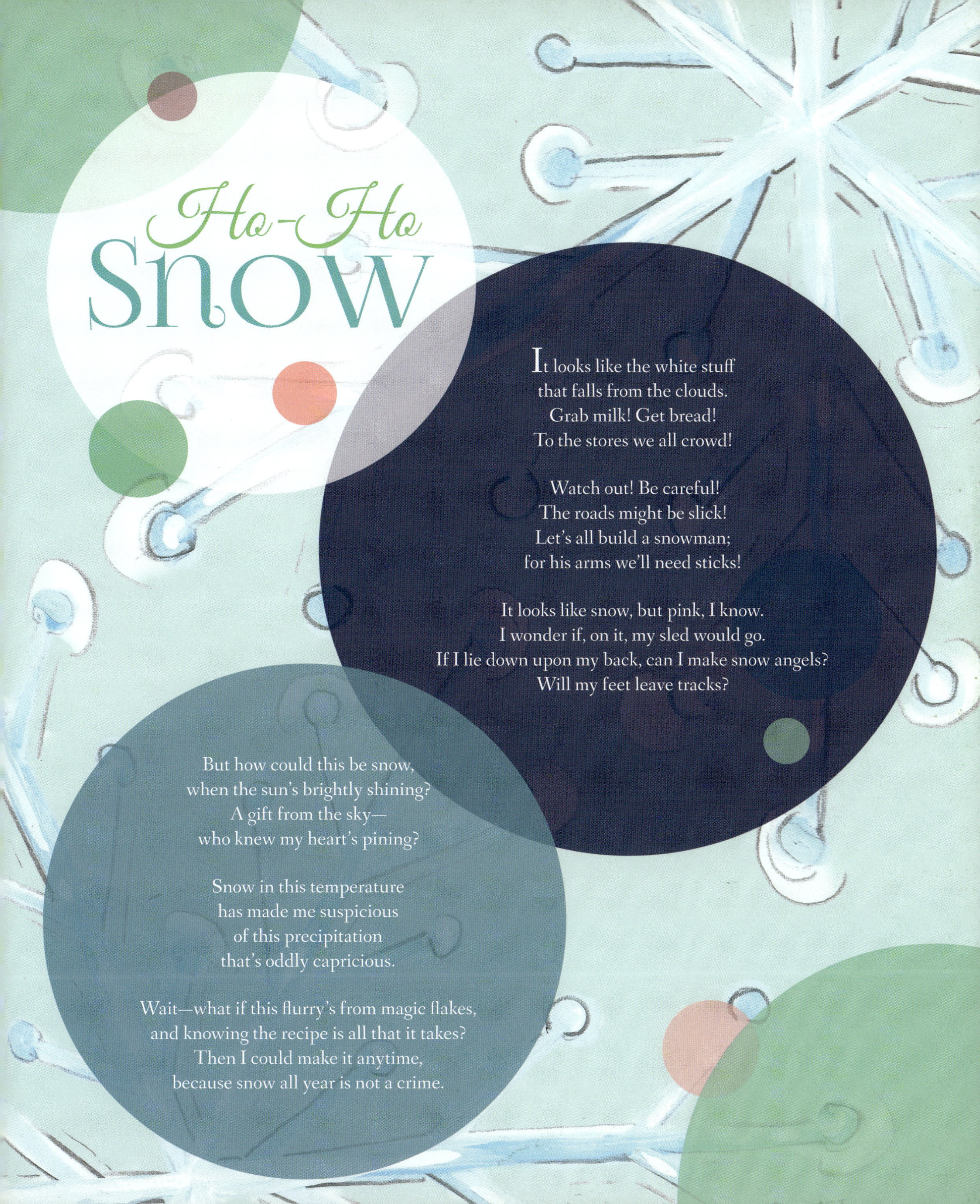

Ho-Ho Snow

It looks like the white stuff
that falls from the clouds.
Grab milk! Get bread!
To the stores we all crowd!

Watch out! Be careful!
The roads might be slick!
Let's all build a snowman;
for his arms we'll need sticks!

It looks like snow, but pink, I know.
I wonder if, on it, my sled would go.
If I lie down upon my back, can I make snow angels?
Will my feet leave tracks?

But how could this be snow,
when the sun's brightly shining?
A gift from the sky—
who knew my heart's pining?

Snow in this temperature
has made me suspicious
of this precipitation
that's oddly capricious.

Wait—what if this flurry's from magic flakes,
and knowing the recipe is all that it takes?
Then I could make it anytime,
because snow all year is not a crime.

Santa's Magic Snow

I'm not really sure if I should reference this project as a craft or a scientific experiment, but if you have kids, they will call it magic! All you need are a few items easily found around the house and eight hours' sleep, then, poof, you have a sparkling snowflake with more facets than the Hope Diamond!

1 Make the base stem of the snowflake. Use scissors to cut an 8½-inch length of hot pink chenille stem. Measure 2 inches from the end of the stem and make a loop by bending the stem and wrapping it around itself, as shown.

2 Use scissors to cut two 6½-inch pieces of hot pink chenille stem. Wrap each piece around the center of the base chenille stem, as shown.

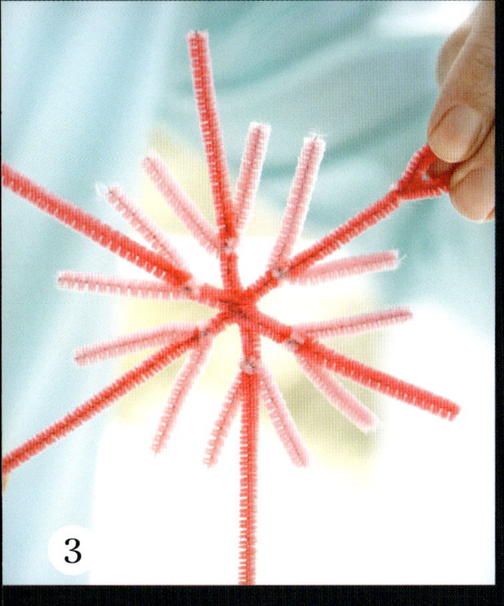

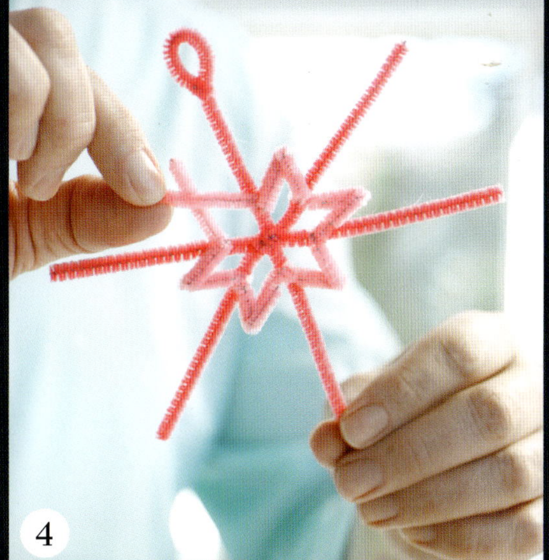

6

3 Use scissors to cut six 3-inch pieces of light pink chenille stem. Wrap one piece around each leg of the snowflake, as shown.

4 Join the light pink chenille stems together by crossing over the adjoining stems to make an X; then bend the ends down, as shown.

5 Use scissors to cut twelve 2-inch pieces of light pink chenille stem and wrap two pieces around each leg of the snowflake, as shown.

6 Find a glass container that is large enough for the snowflake to easily fit inside without touching the sides, top, or bottom when suspended. My snowflake is pretty big, which requires a large container. You could use the same process to make a snowflake that is small enough to fit into a glass jar.

7

8

9

10

7 Position a wooden dowel across the top of the glass container and use a small piece of floral stem wire to hang the snowflake. Set aside.

Steps 8–11 should be done by a supervising adult.

8 Fill the glass container with enough boiling water to completely cover the snowflake, except for the hanging loop, which should remain above the water. It's a good idea to temper the glass container to keep it from breaking when the boiling water is added. Do this by rinsing the container with hot tap water before pouring in the boiling water.

9 Add 3 tablespoons of Borax for each cup of water in the container and stir carefully with a wooden spoon.

10 Slowly lower the snowflake into the Borax and water solution, resting the dowel across the top. The snowflake should hang freely without touching the sides or bottom of the container.

11 Now for the hardest step of all: Leave the container and snowflake untouched for approximately 8 hours, or overnight. If you wiggle or try to peek at the Magic Snow early, it will disrupt the crystal formations that are growing on the snowflake. When you finally lift the dowel, you will see that your plain chenille snowflake is magically covered in faceted, diamond-like "ice" crystals. Dry with a paper towel and add a piece of pretty ribbon for hanging.

Frosty Folly on a Swing

From the time he arrived in a new falling snow,
it was back to the sky that he wanted to go.

The other snowmen were all happy just standing around,
but Folly dreamt of having his feet off the ground!

He watched the new snowflakes falling softly to earth,
and remembered that ride he, too, took at birth.

So he started to think, "What could put me up higher?
Perhaps a tall ladder, standing straight like a spire?

No, that won't work, because my feet won't be free.
But I could get that effect standing in the top of a tree.

Wait—I have an idea that I think might just work.
I'll suspend a striped swing, like a trapeze in the cirque!"

Folly's wish of flying high came true on that day,
which shows if you dream, then your heart finds a way!

Frosty Folly on a Swing

One of the most popular icons of the holiday season is the beloved three-ball stack—a snowman with two lumps of coal and a carrot nose—but I have always wanted more for my frozen friends than perhaps they have even wanted for themselves! When I sat down to make this ornament from the winter wonderland in my mind, my first thought was to get him off that cold hard ground and onto a swing, where he could fly through the air with the greatest of freeze. I followed it with a whole new shape and traded in that old top hat for something more appropriate for a party!

GATHER YOUR GLITTER, SCISSORS, AND GLUE. HERE'S EVERYTHING NEEDED FOR THIS MAKE AND DO!

Materials

- 1-inch-diameter Styrofoam ball
- Paperclay
- Kitchen skewer
- ¼-inch-diameter dowel
- Two 18-inch pieces of 16-gauge floral stem wire
- White floral tape
- Hat Pattern (see page 173)
- Card stock
- White glue
- Acrylic paints
- White photocopier paper
- Toothpick
- Gesso (optional)
- Jacket Patterns (see page 173)
- 18-inch piece of 18-gauge floral stem wire
- Swing Frame Template (see page 173)
- Medium-weight cardboard
- Glitter
- 1½ × ½ × ½-inch block of balsa wood
- Pink card stock
- Ribbon (optional)

Tools

- Short length of ¼-inch-diameter dowel
- Pencil sharpener
- New #2 pencil with eraser
- Easy Cutter tool or hacksaw
- Ruler
- Wire cutters
- Drill with 1/16-inch bit
- Craft knife
- Photocopier
- Scissors
- Paintbrushes
- Self-healing mat
- Fine-grade sandpaper (220 grit)
- Needle-nose pliers
- Hot glue gun
- Holly craft punch (optional)

1 Make the head. Place the Styrofoam ball in the center of a flattened circle of Paperclay. Dipping the Styrofoam ball into water before applying the clay will help the clay to stick better.

2 Pull the Paperclay up around the ball. Work the air bubbles out of the opening before squeezing the clay shut.

3 Gently roll the ball between your hands until it is even and smooth. This should be with the amount of pressure you would use if it were a raw egg in its shell.

4 Carefully push the ball onto the end of a ¼-inch-diameter dowel that has been sharpened with a pencil sharpener. This dowel will only be used as a holder. Be careful not to push it all the way through, and try not to misshape the roundness of the ball during the process. With the eraser end of a new #2 pencil, gently make indentations in the clay for the eyes.

5 Use an Easy Cutter tool or wire cutters to cut a 1-inch piece from the pointed end of a kitchen skewer and insert it into the face for the nose. Set the head aside and allow the Paperclay to harden.

6 Make the torso of the figure. Use an Easy Cutter tool or hacksaw to cut a piece of ¼-inch-diameter dowel to a length of approximately 3 inches.

7 Use a pencil to mark the placement of the arms and legs, approximately ½ inch from the top of the torso for the arms, and ¼ inch from

8
9
10
11
12
13
14
15
16

8 Use a drill with a 1/16-inch bit to drill holes all the way through the dowel at each of the places you marked. Insert one 18-inch piece of 16-gauge floral stem wire through each hole. Bend the wires down, as shown. Keep the wires in place by wrapping with floral tape.

9 Wrap the dowel, arms, and legs with floral tape.

10 Roll a 1½-inch-diameter ball of Paperclay and cut it in half with a craft knife. Moisten both halves with water and put them back together around the bottom of the dowel as shown. Blend the edges back together with your fingers.

11 Wrap a flattened rectangle of Paperclay around the dowel above the ball.

12 Blend the two shapes together with your fingers until they resemble an oddly shaped pear. Set aside to allow the Paperclay to harden.

13 Make the hat. Copy the Hat Pattern on card stock. Use scissors to cut it out. Roll it into a cone and secure the seam with white glue. Paint the hat and allow it to dry.

14 Cut a 4- × 3/8-inch strip of white paper and fringe both sides with scissors. Attach the fringed band to the bottom of the hat with white glue. Fringe an additional 1- × 3/8-inch strip of white paper. Twirl it around the end of a toothpick and secure it with white glue. Insert the fringed toothpick into the top of the cone and secure it with white glue. Do not trim the toothpick because it will be used later to attach the hat to the head. Set aside.

15 Sand the figure and head lightly until the Paperclay is smooth. Brush the entire figure and head with gesso or white acrylic paint and allow to dry. Place the head on the figure and secure it with white glue. Use a pencil to lightly sketch the face before painting. Be careful not to draw too heavily because the lead can smudge and muddy your paint. If this should happen, just use a damp paper towel to remove it.

16 Use a small brush to paint the details of the face. Set aside to dry.

17 Paint the arms and body of his festive jacket as shown. Set aside to dry.

17

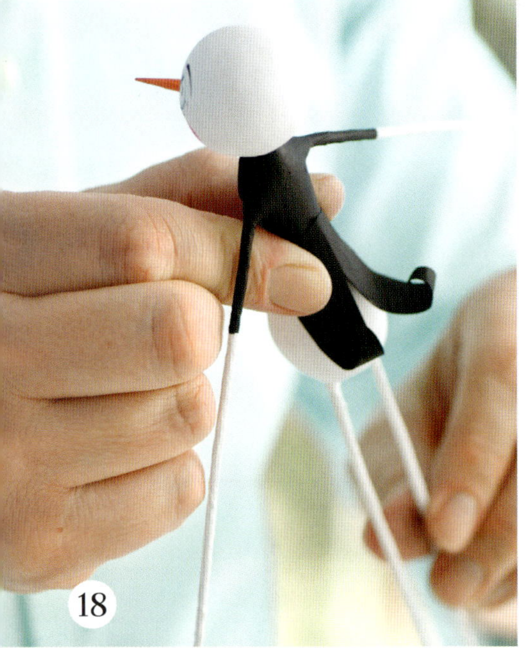
18

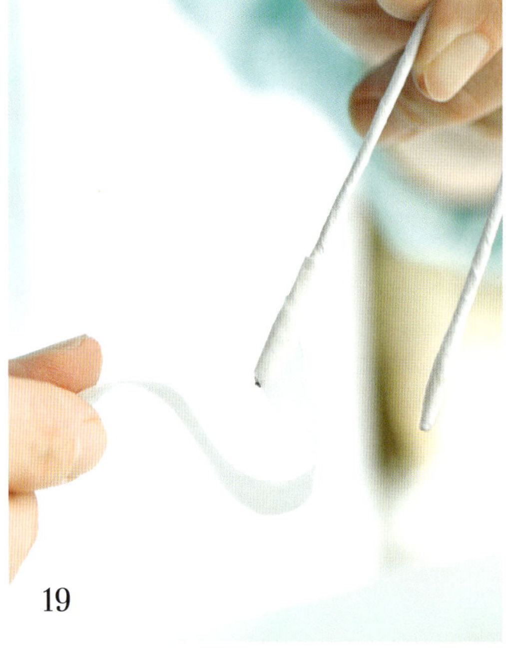
19

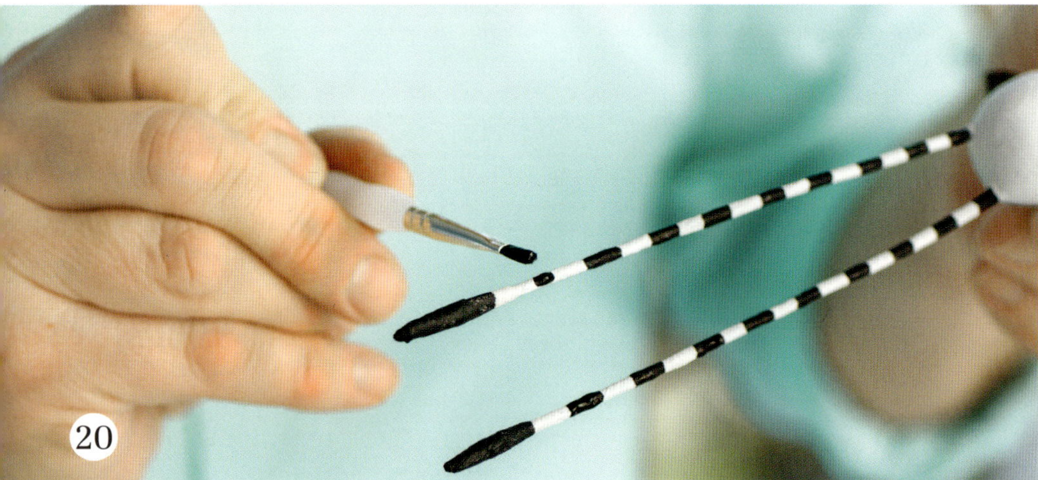
20

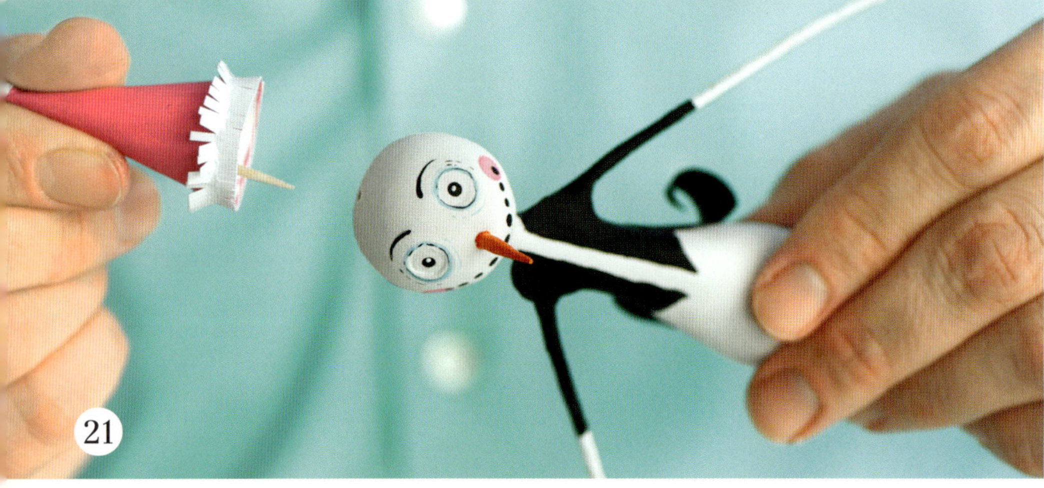
21

18 Make the jacket. Copy the jacket patterns on card stock and use scissors to cut them out. Paint the lapels and tails black, allow them to dry, and then attach them to the figure with white glue.

19 Use wire cutters to trim the legs to a length of approximately 5½ inches. Wrap approximately ½ inch at the end of each leg with a couple of layers of floral tape and squeeze to look like shoes.

20 Stripe the legs using a small flat brush; then paint the shoes. Allow to dry.

21 Drill a small hole in the top of the head. Position the party hat on top of the head and insert the toothpick into the hole by pushing firmly from the top of the fringed toothpick.

22 Wrap an 18-inch piece of 18-gauge floral stem wire with floral tape. Paint the wire with a pink base coat and allow to dry. Use a small brush to add red stripes and allow to dry.

23 Make the swing. Copy the Swing Frame Templates on card stock and bend the wire to match the wire template. Be careful not to overwork the wire.

24 Use a craft knife to cut a 4¼- × 1¼-inch rectangle out of medium-weight cardboard or use the Swing Frame Seat Template as your guide. Use a drill to make a hole in the center of each end, ⅛ inch from the end, as shown. This will be the seat of the swing. Paint the seat pink and allow it to dry.

25 Insert the ends of the swing frame through the holes on the seat and use needle-nose pliers to bend up ½ inch on each side. Secure the ends of the wire with hot glue.

22

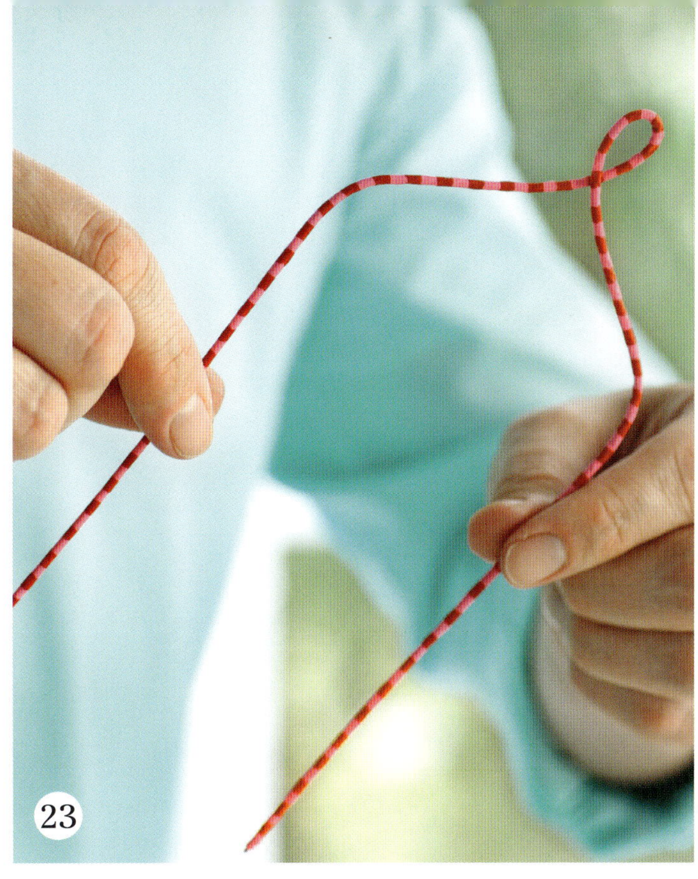
23

24

25

26

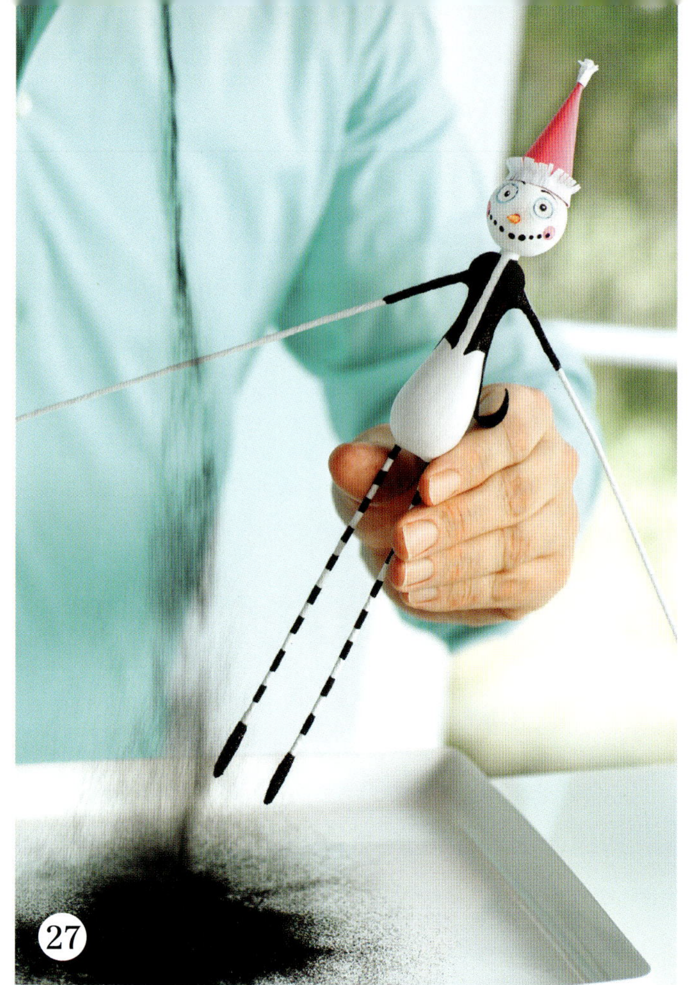
27

28

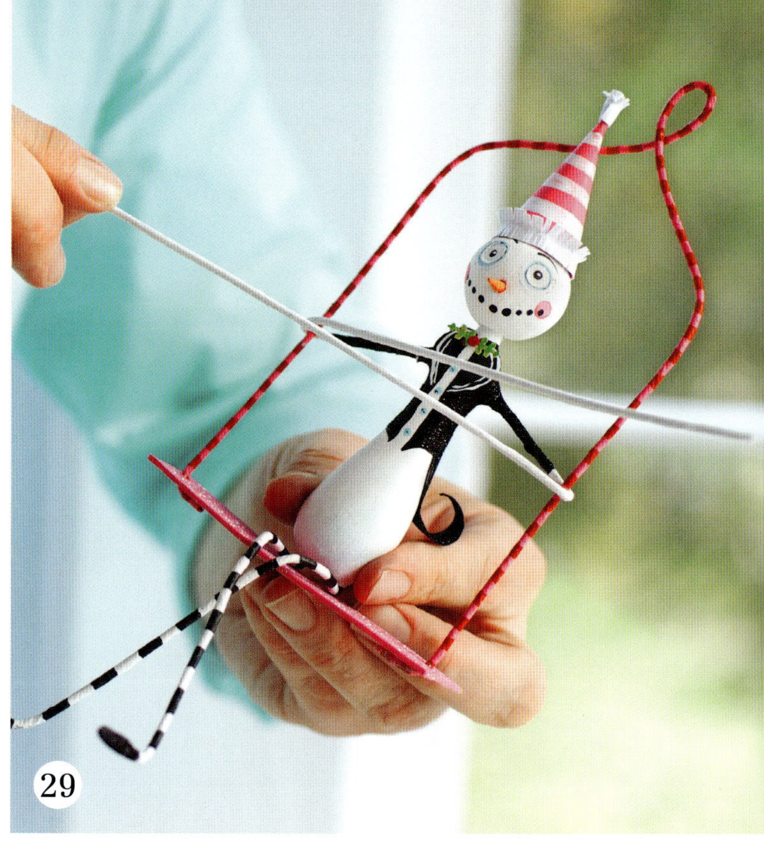
29

26 Brush the seat of the swing with white glue and sprinkle with pink glitter.

27 Add sparkle to the jacket and shoes by brushing both with white glue and sprinkling with black glitter. Do not glitter the lapels of the jacket.

28 Use a small brush to add white details to the lapels of the jacket and a flat brush to add stripes to the party hat. Allow to dry. Make the bow tie. Cut or punch a holly sprig out of card stock and use a small brush to add details. Attach the bow tie with white glue.

29 Position the figure on the swing and bend the arms and legs, as shown.

30 After wrapping the arms around the sides of the swing, use a pair of wire cutters to trim the excess wire. Use the center of Frosty's body as your guide. It should look as if his hands are touching each other in front of him.

31 Make the package. Drill a hole straight through the center of the small balsa wood block. Paint it and allow it to dry. Use strips of pink card stock to make a paper bow, and attach it with white glue. Insert the ends of the arm wires into the holes on both sides of the package and secure them with a small drop of white glue. Add a piece of ribbon for hanging, and he's ready to go!

30

31

Had A Very Glittered Nose!

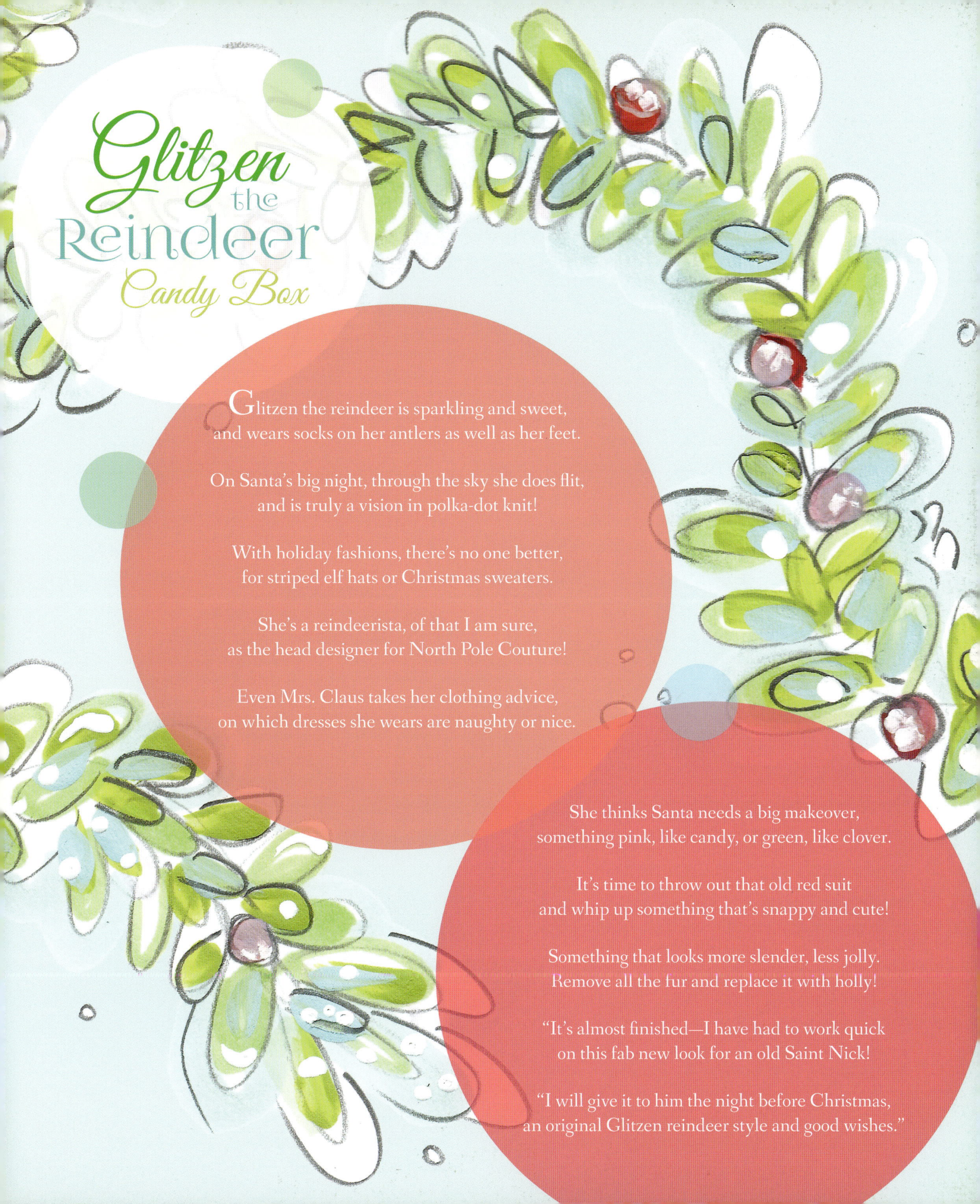

Glitzen the Reindeer Candy Box

Glitzen the reindeer is sparkling and sweet,
and wears socks on her antlers as well as her feet.

On Santa's big night, through the sky she does flit,
and is truly a vision in polka-dot knit!

With holiday fashions, there's no one better,
for striped elf hats or Christmas sweaters.

She's a reindeerista, of that I am sure,
as the head designer for North Pole Couture!

Even Mrs. Claus takes her clothing advice,
on which dresses she wears are naughty or nice.

She thinks Santa needs a big makeover,
something pink, like candy, or green, like clover.

It's time to throw out that old red suit
and whip up something that's snappy and cute!

Something that looks more slender, less jolly.
Remove all the fur and replace it with holly!

"It's almost finished—I have had to work quick
on this fab new look for an old Saint Nick!

"I will give it to him the night before Christmas,
an original Glitzen reindeer style and good wishes."

Glitzen the Reindeer Candy Box

I love giving handmade gifts during the holidays. One of my favorites for gifting and getting is homemade candy in a fabulously decorated box. Although fancy packages were once the norm for delivering treats, you rarely see that kind of attention to detail today just for holding something you eat. The person for whom you make this glittering Glitzen box will get not only a wacky and wonderful decoration, but also a sweet surprise inside!

Make and do! Gather your glitter, scissors, and glue. Here's everything needed for this make and do!

Materials

- Two 3-inch-diameter Styrofoam balls
- Kitchen skewer
- Paperclay
- Acrylic paints
- Antler Art (page 174)
- Card stock
- White glue
- Toothpicks
- Ear Pattern (page 174)
- Dark brown felt
- Light brown felt
- Glitter
- White floral tape
- Heavy-weight cardboard
- Gesso (optional)
- 4-inch-diameter round craft box
- Red flocking powder (optional)
- Aluminum foil
- Paper festooning (see page xxiii)
- Two jingle bells
- White regular chenille stem
- White marabou
- Banner Art (page 174)

Tools

- Felt-tip marker
- Clay-sculpting tool
- Fine-grade sandpaper (220 grit)
- Paintbrushes
- Photocopier
- Scissors
- Pencil
- Craft knife (optional)
- Ruler
- Drill with 1⁄16-inch bit
- Pinking shears
- Flexible measuring tape
- Serrated knife
- Hot glue gun
- Wire cutters

1 Make the head. Use the end of a felt-tip marker or your thumb to make an indentation in one of the Styrofoam balls for the mouth.

2 Insert a kitchen skewer into the bottom of the Styrofoam ball to make it easier to hold while you sculpt and paint. This skewer will be used later in the project, so make sure it is straight and centered in the ball. Dip the Styrofoam ball in water to moisten it lightly. Wetting the Styrofoam helps the Paperclay adhere better. Make several medium-sized flat pieces of Paperclay and begin to cover the ball. Press Paperclay into the mouth indentation and continue blending and smoothing with your fingers until the entire ball is evenly covered.

3 Add three small balls of Paperclay to the face to create the eyelids and nose. Blend and shape with your fingers. Use a clay-sculpting tool to add detail to the mouth and nose. Allow the Paperclay to harden and sand lightly with fine-grade sandpaper.

4 Paint the head (except for the eyes, nose, and mouth) with a base coat of brown acrylic paint and allow it to dry. Color block the eyes, nose, and mouth. Use a small detail brush to paint the eyebrows, lips, and teeth.

5 Make the antlers. Copy the Antler Art on card stock and use scissors to cut it out. Use a pencil to trace the indicated number of pieces on card stock and cut them out with scissors or a craft knife. Glue the front and back pieces of each antler together, sandwiching a toothpick between them with approximately ½ inch sticking out, as shown. The toothpicks will be used to attach the antlers to the head.

6 Make the ears. Copy the Ear Pattern pieces on card stock and use scissors to cut them out. Use a felt-tip marker to trace the pattern pieces onto dark brown and light brown felt, as indicated, and cut them out with scissors. Glue the pieces together, sandwiching a toothpick between the layers with approximately ½ inch sticking out, as shown.

4

5

6

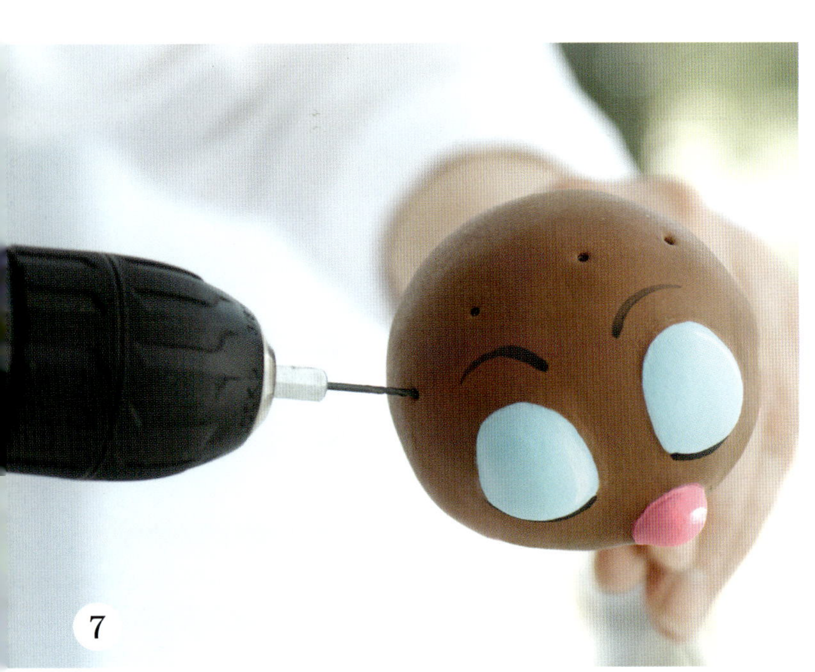
7

8

9

10

7 Use a drill with a 1⁄16-inch bit to make four holes in the top of the head, as shown.

8 Attach the ears and antlers by dipping the toothpick ends in white glue and inserting them into the holes in the top of the head, as shown.

9 Brush the eyes, antlers, nose, and teeth with white glue and sprinkle with glitter.

10 Wrap the kitchen skewer with two even layers of white floral tape. Base coat the wrapped skewer with white acrylic paint and allow it to dry. Add pink and red stripes, beginning just below the head and continuing ¾ of the length of the skewer. The bottom will be trimmed off later, so there's no need to stripe it. Set aside.

11 Make the box. Use card stock to make a 4½-inch-diameter circle pattern and cut it out with scissors. Trace two circles onto heavyweight cardboard and use pinking shears to cut them out. Coat both circles, front and back, with gesso or white acrylic paint and set aside to dry.

12 Coat the entire craft box with gesso or white acrylic paint and allow it to dry. Wrap a flexible measuring tape around the box and make a small pencil mark at the beginning and at the halfway point. Continue dividing each section in half and marking until you get the width stripes you want. Use a ruler to draw the stripes from the top to the bottom. For my 4-inch-diameter box, the stripes are approximately ¾ inch wide.

13 Coat the bottom of the box with white glue and attach one of the circles. Allow to dry completely. Paint the marked sections of the box, alternating pink and red. Allow to dry.

14

15

16

14 Brush the stripes and bottom edge of the box with white glue and sprinkle with glitter or flocking powder. Coat the top of the box with white glue and attach the second circle. Allow to dry completely. Brush the top with white glue and sprinkle with glitter.

15 Make the base for the head. Use a serrated knife to cut a Styrofoam ball in half. Brush one of the halves with white glue and sandwich it between two pieces of aluminum foil. Carefully smooth the foil over the rounded side of the half-ball. Trim the edges, leaving approximately ¼-inch allowance and fold it under the flat side. Carefully insert the skewer halfway into the flat bottom of the half-ball to serve as a handle during painting and glittering. Paint the domed top of the half-ball with white acrylic paint and allow to dry. Add stripes and allow to dry. Brush the half-ball with white glue and sprinkle it with glitter. Carefully remove the skewer when the glitter is dry. Reserve the second half of the ball for future use.

16 Fold a piece of paper festooning into a circle the size of the top of the box and use hot glue to attach it.

17 Use hot glue to attach the base of the half-ball in the center of the festooning. Use a toothpick or your fingers to gently pick the layers of festooning open.

18 Use wire cutters to trim the skewer to approximately 5½ inches in length. Push it straight down into the top of the half-ball base. If it wobbles, shim it with a piece of toothpick pushed in beside the skewer. Add a small amount of white glue to secure.

19 Thread two jingle bells onto a piece of white chenille stem and wrap it around the skewer, just below the head. Use hot glue to attach a 2½-inch-long piece of white marabou above the bells to cover the chenille.

20 Copy the Banner Art on card stock and use scissors or a craft knife to cut it out. Stripe two toothpicks, allow them to dry, and use white glue to attach them to the banner. Center the banner and push the toothpicks into the base as shown. Optional: For extra dazzle, glue on black strips of paper for eyelashes.

Ginger Cookie Kids

There's a yummy place
that's at the North Pole.
It's Santa's bakery,
called Sprinkles on Snow!

Inside this frosted palace place
are cookies wearing bow ties and lace.
It's like a workshop where elves make toys,
but here it's gingersnap girls and boys.

Mrs. Claus is quickly rolling out dough,
where soon the cookie shapes will go.
In leaps, a reindeer with shoes made like cutters,
stamps out the cookies, both sugar and butter!

There's also an elf with a spatula in hand,
who flips up the cookies that land on a pan.
There they'll get dusted with ginger and spice.
Two shakes for the boys, to make sure they are nice.

Now into the oven they go with a dash,
to be painted by pixies—golden brown, should you ask!
What seemed no sooner than when they had begun,
jingle bells signaled the cookies were done.

Then, from the oven, there came a bright glow,
and out came the gingers to put on a show.
From the tips of their toes to the tops of their heads,
they were covered in frostings both piped and spread.

Come on, little cookie treats,
it's time to visit the land of sweets!
It won't be long 'til you're on your way,
traveling the world in Santa's sleigh.

1

2

Ginger Cookie Kids

Nothing is more magical than a tree covered in yummy treats for the holiday season. Through the years, I've made hundreds of cookie ornaments using different kinds of clay, homemade salt doughs, etc. None were as successful as the methods described in this project, which uses Styrofoam as a base. When the Styrofoam is painted, small holes and crevices start to appear, making it look so real that you can almost smell cookies baking!

1 Make the cookies. Copy the Gingerbread Styrofoam Patterns on card stock and use scissors to cut them out. Use a felt-tip marker to trace the cookie shapes onto a ½-inch-thick sheet of Styrofoam.

3

4

5

6

2 Place the sheet of Styrofoam on a self-healing mat, or other protected surface, and carefully cut out the cookie shapes with a sharp craft knife.

3 Lightly sand around the edges of the Styrofoam to make it more rounded, like a real baked cookie.

4 Paint the cookies with a base coat of dark brown acrylic paint to look like gingerbread, and set them aside to dry.

5 Copy the Body Patterns on card stock and use scissors to cut them out. Use a felt-tip marker to trace them onto tan felt, and cut them out with scissors.

6 Brush a light coat of white glue onto the cookies and attach the felt body pieces.

7

7 Copy the Cheek and Eye Pattern pieces and Clothing Pattern pieces on card stock and use scissors to cut them out. Use a felt-tip marker to trace all of the pieces onto felt and then cut them out with scissors. Glue on the eyes. Stack the pieces, starting with white, then the blue iris, followed by the black pupil on top.

8 Glue on the rosy pink cheeks.

9 Create the mouth by pushing sequin pins through the felt halfway into the Styrofoam in the shape of a smile.

10 Paint the heads of the sequin pins with red acrylic paint and allow to dry.

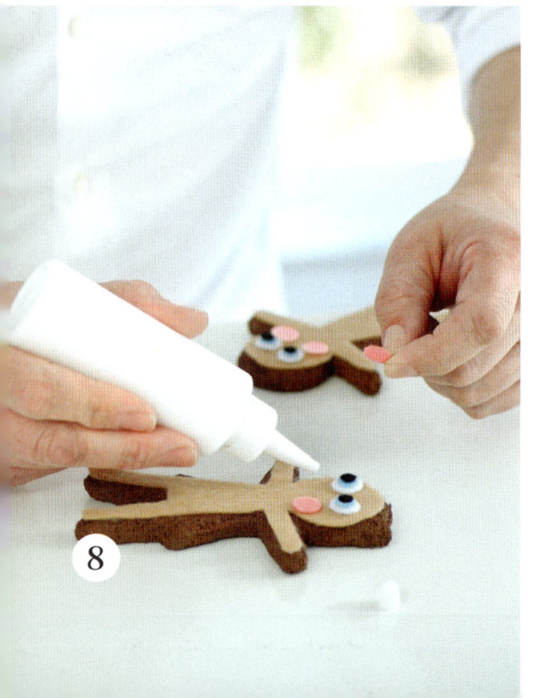

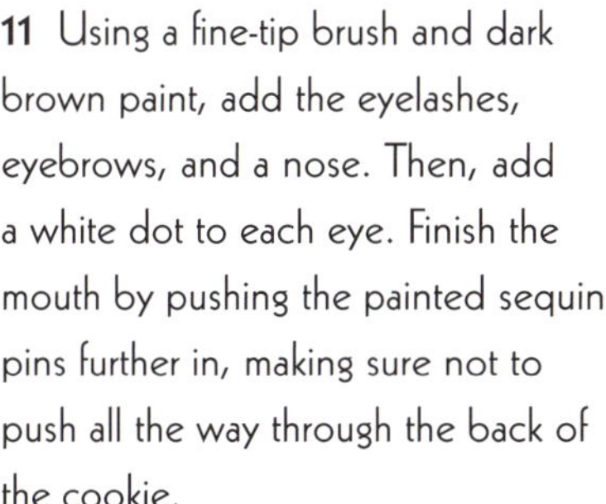

11

12

13

11 Using a fine-tip brush and dark brown paint, add the eyelashes, eyebrows, and a nose. Then, add a white dot to each eye. Finish the mouth by pushing the painted sequin pins further in, making sure not to push all the way through the back of the cookie.

12 Use white glue to attach the clothing pieces, as shown.

13 Decorate the Ginger Cookie Kids with pieces of small chenille stems that have been shaped with your fingers to resemble cookie icing and attach with white glue. If you want to use them as ornaments, push a small loop of wire into the tops and secure with white glue. Add baker's twine or ribbon for hanging.

Oh So Sweet!

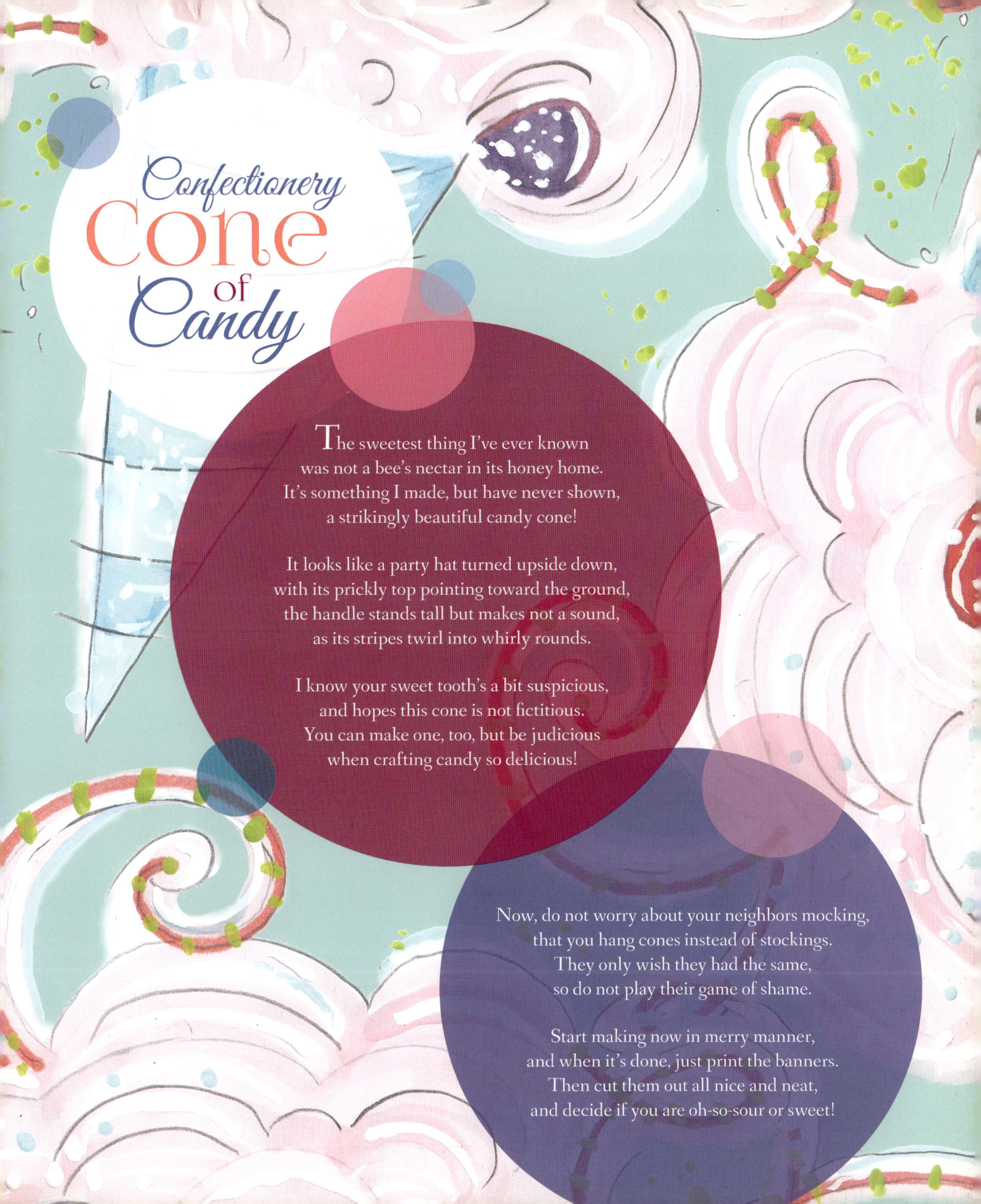

Confectionery Cone of Candy

The sweetest thing I've ever known
was not a bee's nectar in its honey home.
It's something I made, but have never shown,
a strikingly beautiful candy cone!

It looks like a party hat turned upside down,
with its prickly top pointing toward the ground,
the handle stands tall but makes not a sound,
as its stripes twirl into whirly rounds.

I know your sweet tooth's a bit suspicious,
and hopes this cone is not fictitious.
You can make one, too, but be judicious
when crafting candy so delicious!

Now, do not worry about your neighbors mocking,
that you hang cones instead of stockings.
They only wish they had the same,
so do not play their game of shame.

Start making now in merry manner,
and when it's done, just print the banners.
Then cut them out all nice and neat,
and decide if you are oh-so-sour or sweet!

Confectionery Cone of Candy

Learning to make a perfect cone from card stock or poster board is one of the more essential skills in my studio. Not only is it the base for making party hats, it's the key ingredient in making this two-sided treat cone that can be easily flipped to change the status of someone's holiday behavior from "Oh So Sweet" to "Oh So Sour"! I like to hang these instead of traditional stockings so Santa knows right away that I've been sweet!

GATHER YOUR GLITTER, SCISSORS, AND GLUE. HERE'S EVERYTHING NEEDED FOR THIS MAKE AND DO!

Materials

- Cone Art (page 176)
- Card stock
- White glue
- Red flocking powder
- Pink flocking powder
- Iridescent glitter
- Frosting Art (page 177)
- 18-inch piece of 18-gauge floral stem wire
- White floral tape
- Acrylic paints
- Paper Festooning (see page xxiii) or pleated crepe paper
- Oh So Sweet Banner (page 176)
- Oh So Sour Banner (page 176)
- Candy and Lemon Art (page 176)
- 22-gauge floral stem wire
- Painted toothpicks

Tools

- Photocopier
- Scissors
- Paintbrushes
- Hot glue gun
- Ruler
- Hole punch
- Round-nose pliers
- Wire cutters
- Toothpick (optional)

1 Make the cone. Copy the Cone Art on card stock and use scissors to cut it out. Use white glue to attach the two pieces together, creating a half circle.

2 Roll the half circle into a cone and secure the seam with white glue. Carefully match up the stripes at the seam. Allow the glue to dry completely.

3 Brush the red stripes with white glue and sprinkle with red flocking powder. Allow to dry. Brush the pink stripes with white glue and sprinkle with pink flocking powder. Allow to dry. Brush the white stripes with white glue and sprinkle with iridescent glitter. Allow to dry.

4 Make the frosting. Copy the Frosting Art on card stock and use scissors to cut out the pieces. To add dimension, apply a line of hot glue around the edges of both pieces of frosting.

5 Use glue dots to attach the blue layer of frosting to the cone, as shown. Use the bottom of the top stripe as a guide.

6 Use glue dots to attach the white frosting around the top of the cone.

7 Use a hole punch to make a hole through all the layers, on both sides of the cone, approximately ¼ inch from the top of the cone

8 Make the handle. Wrap an 18-inch piece of 18-gauge floral stem wire with white floral tape and brush with white acrylic paint. Allow to dry. Bring both ends of the wire toward the center, and cross to create a loop, as shown.

9 Create a loop approximately 2 inches from each end of the wire as shown. Be careful not to overwork the wire.

10 Insert the ends of the wire through the holes on each side of the cone and use round-nose pliers to bend over the ends, attaching the handle to the cone.

11 Use acrylic paints and a small brush to add stripes to the handle.

12 Brush the white frosting with white glue and sprinkle with iridescent glitter. Allow to dry.

13 Use scissors to trim a piece of paper festooning to fit around the inside edge of the cone and use hot glue to secure it.

10

11

12

13

14
15
Oh So Sweet!
16
17

14 Use your fingers or a toothpick to carefully separate the layers of the paper festooning to create a ruffle.

15 Make the banners. Copy the Oh So Sweet and Oh So Sour banners on card stock and use scissors to cut them out. Use hot glue to attach the banners, back to back, on the handle, sandwiching the wire between the two pieces.

16 Make the candies and lemon slices. Copy the Candy and Lemon Art on card stock and use scissors to cut out the pieces. Use wire cutters to cut two 3-inch pieces of 22-gauge floral stem wire. Brush the backs of the candy and lemon pieces with white glue and sandwich the end of the wire between them. Each wire should have a lemon on one side and a candy on the other.

17 Brush the candy, lemon slices, and edges of the banners with white glue and sprinkle with iridescent glitter. Use acrylic paints and a small brush to add stripes to the candy and lemon wires and allow to dry. Attach the candy and lemon pieces by wrapping the end of each wire around the curled wire at the sides of the cone handle. Be sure that the candy and lemon pieces correspond with the banner at the top when attaching.

18 Make the sprinkles. Use wire cutters to cut painted toothpicks into ⅜-inch-long pieces. Use white glue to attach the sprinkles to the frosting.

Nutty as a Fruitcake!

Nutty as a Fruitcake Party Hat

The holidays herald a whole lot of things
that make birds, teapots, and carolers sing.
But with this merriment they also bring
the kooky kinfolk, whom you have rarely seen.

We all have a family member possessing a unique style and flair,
so worry not if you've got one—I don't judge and don't care.
In fact, I'll take this time to share,
about an aunt of mine who's really "rare."

In months one through eleven we hear not a word
from this unusual woman, referred to as our "Auntie Absurd."
But, just as the calendar days count down through December,
there's a knock at the door, and in steps our family's merriest member!

She arrives with an invisible elf on her shoulder,
whom she talks to and interprets, "He wishes it colder."
"He's from the North Pole," she says, "so it makes perfect sense,"
and announces it's about time that this dinner commence!

We all look around, without giggles or grins,
as she peeks for the place-carded seat of her friend,
then states, "I can't believe that it's happened again,
no seat for poor Charlie, whom you assume I pretend."

Her exit is timely, just as it is every year.
At this point, if she stayed, it'd be a first—and plain weird.
Someone always jokes that our auntie is only half-baked,
and every head nods in agreement; she's a nutty fruitcake!

Nutty as a Fruitcake Party Hat

Let's be honest: The holidays make us all just a little bit crazier than we may or may not be the rest of the year. So instead of letting everyone figure out for themselves that you might be a few stripes shy of a candy cane, just embrace it and warn them yourself with a party hat that tells the whole story. After all, if they're going to talk about you behind your back anyway, let it be about how creative you are!

Materials

- White poster board
- White glue
- Gesso (optional)
- Acrylic paints
- Red flocking powder
- Glitter
- Satin ribbon
- Paper Festooning (page xxiii)
- Marabou
- Kitchen skewer
- 3-inch-diameter Styrofoam ball
- Medium-weight cardboard
- Round-headed pins
- Textured snow paint
- Glasses Art (page 177)
- Card stock
- Styrofoam scraps
- Toothpicks
- 20-gauge floral stem wire
- Small chenille stems
- Regular chenille stems
- 2-inch-diameter Styrofoam balls
- Fruitcake Banner Art (page 177)

Tools

- Pencil
- Scissors
- Paintbrushes
- Ruler
- Hole punch
- Craft knife
- Hot glue gun
- Wire cutters
- Serrated knife
- Felt-tip marker
- Quarter (or other 1-inch-diameter coin)
- 1/8-inch hole punch
- Kitchen skewer
- New #2 pencil with eraser
- Photocopier
- Wire cutters

1 Make the hat. Follow the instructions in the Glitter Guide for making a 9-inch party hat cone out of poster board (see page xxi). Base coat the cone with gesso or white acrylic paint and allow it to dry. Mark stripes with a pencil and paint with acrylics. Allow to dry.

2 Brush the red stripes with white glue and sprinkle with red flocking powder. Allow to dry.

3 Brush the pink stripes with white glue and sprinkle with glitter. Allow to dry.

4 Use a hole punch to make a hole at the bottom on each side of the cone, approximately ¼ inch from the edge. If you don't have a punch, just cut a small X with your craft knife.

5 Use scissors to cut two pieces of satin ribbon approximately 24 inches long. Put one ribbon through each hole and tie a knot inside the cone to secure.

6 Use a hot glue gun to attach a piece of paper festooning around the bottom of the cone. Start and stop in the back, so the seam doesn't show. Following the stitch line in the center of the festooning as a guide, attach a piece of marabou all the way around using hot glue.

7 Use wire cutters to trim a kitchen skewer to approximately 5 inches. Insert the skewer through the top of the hat from the inside. Leave approximately 1 inch protruding from the top and with hot glue secure the other end on the inside. This is where Miss Fruitcake will be attached when she is completed.

8 Make Miss Fruitcake's body. Use a serrated knife to trim a slice off of the top and bottom of a 3-inch-diameter Styrofoam ball, as shown.

9 Using a felt-tip marker (or something similar) as a shaper, press on the sides in an up-and-down motion as you turn the Styrofoam in your hand. You are creating eight segments similar to those in a Bundt cake.

10 Continue shaping the fruitcake by pressing into the top with your thumb.

11 Use a quarter to make a circular indentation in the bottom of the Styrofoam fruitcake shape.

12 Use a pencil to trace the quarter onto a piece of medium-weight cardboard. It should be approximately 1 inch diameter. Use scissors to cut out the circle and make a hole in the center with a ⅛-inch hole punch.

13 Brush the cardboard circle with white glue and insert it into the indentation you made in the bottom of the Styrofoam.

10

11

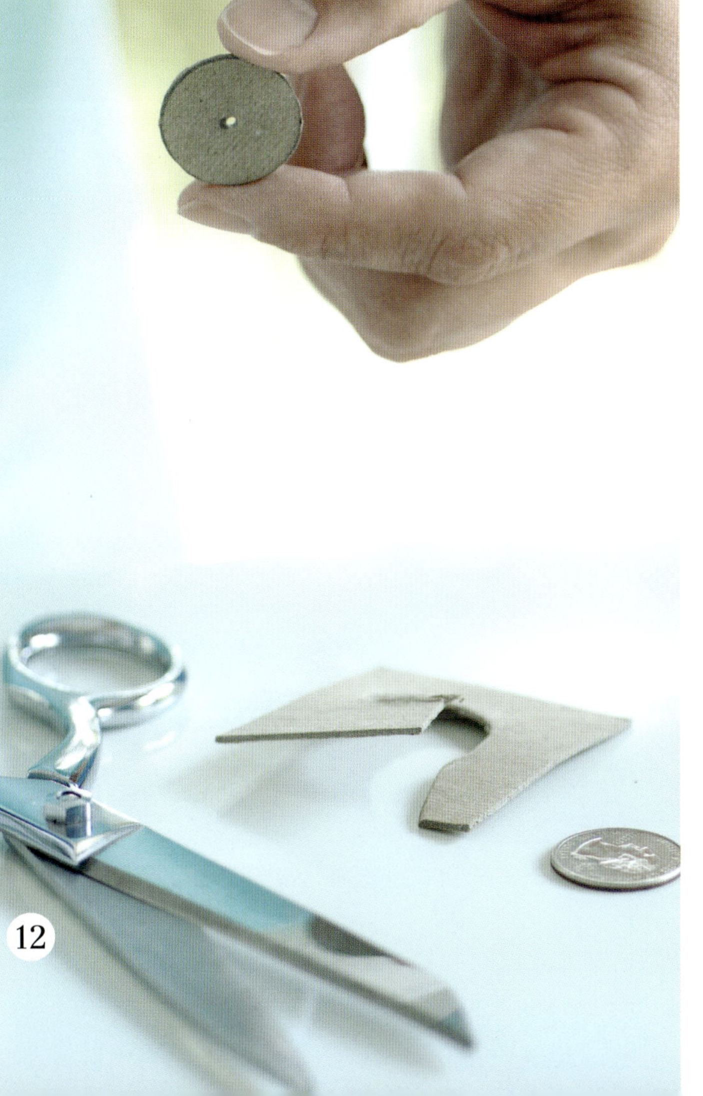
12

13

14 Dust all the loose crumbs off of the fruitcake. Insert a kitchen skewer into the top of the fruitcake to be used as a holder while you paint.

15 Brush the fruitcake with a base coat of brown acrylic paint and allow it to dry. It will take several coats to cover evenly. The porousness of the painted Styrofoam will resemble the texture of cake. When the base coat is completely dry, add the shading details and allow to dry.

16 With the eraser end of a new #2 pencil, make indentations for the eyes, then paint them white. Paint two round-headed pins blue and push one into each of the eye indentations.

17 For the mouth, paint three round-headed pins red and insert them as shown. Finish the painted details of the eyes and mouth.

18 Add a dollop of textured snow paint to the top center of the fruitcake to look like whipped cream. Set aside and allow to dry.

20

21

19 Make the glasses. Copy the Glasses Art on card stock and use a craft knife to cut them out. Brush the back center of the glasses with white glue and attach to the face, as shown.

20 Make the fruit. Use a craft knife to cut Styrofoam scraps into pear, apple, and lemon shapes. Use your fingers to continue shaping the fruit. Add stems to the pear and apple by inserting a toothpick into the top of each of the fruit pieces and using wire cutters to trim to length.

21 Use wire cutters to cut three 3-inch lengths of 20-gauge floral stem wire. Brush with white acrylic paint and allow to dry. Dip the ends of the wires into white glue and insert one wire into the bottom of each of the fruits. Use acrylic paints to add color and shading to the fruit. Allow to dry. Brush the fruit with white glue and sprinkle with iridescent glitter. Allow to dry. Use scissors to cut a small leaf from a scrap of card stock and use white glue to attach it to the top of the apple.

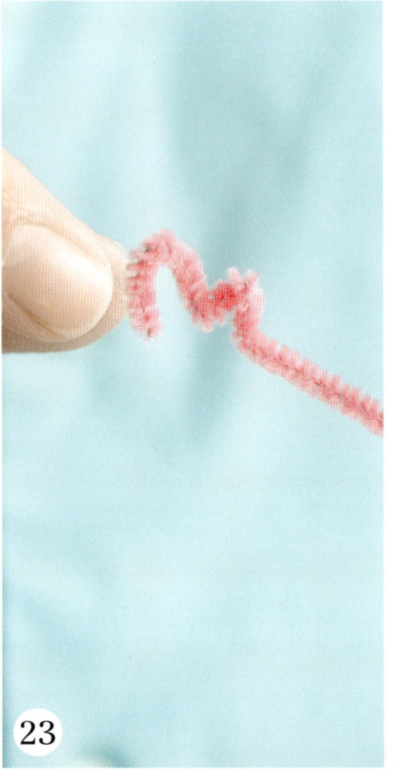

24

25

26

22 Dip the ends of the fruit wires in white glue and stick them into the top of the whipped cream. Use your fingers to bend the wires and arrange the fruits. Add stripes and allow to dry.

23 Make the arms. Use wire cutters to cut one small chenille stem into two equal pieces. Use your fingers to bend one end of each of the small chenille stems into a mitten, as shown.

24 Dip the end of each arm in white glue and insert the arms into the sides of the fruitcake. Bend into shape.

25 Make the legs. Twist two regular chenille stems together and insert them into the bottom of the fruitcake and bend into shape. Fold the ends up for feet and wrap with small chenille stems to look like shoes.

26 Attach Miss Fruitcake to the hat by dipping the protruding skewer into white glue and pushing it into the hole in the bottom of the fruitcake. Be careful not to push all the way through to the top.

27
28

27 Wrap a small piece of marabou around the top of the cone where the fruitcake is attached and secure it with hot glue.

28 Make additional glittered fruits and balls to go around the bottom of the hat. Use a craft knife to shape 2-inch-diameter Styrofoam balls into fruits and continue shaping with your fingers. Place them on 20-gauge floral stem wires. Paint and glitter them, then stripe the wires. Allow to dry.

29 Arrange the glittered fruits around the bottom of the hat. Bend the wires into shape and secure them with hot glue. Copy the Fruitcake Banner Art on card stock. Use scissors or a craft knife to cut it out and use hot glue to attach it.

Glitter Pixies

Do you ever find glitter that's stuck to your face,
but you haven't used any, and there's none in the place?

Where's this sporadic sparkle from?
The source erratic from which it comes?

It's spread by pixies who think it's fun
to sprinkle you when the day's begun.

When you sit down to take off your shoes,
your socks bedazzle like glitter that's glued.

They fling it here, they sling it there.
It's everywhere—they do not care.

Glitter Pixies want *you* to twinkle and shine
without giving the option for your decline.

But they are very helpful sprites,
who do their work both day and night.

So learn to love their glittered ways,
and the sparkle they bring your holidays!

Glitter Pixies

I'm sure that I am not the only one who's noticed that everything around us seems to sparkle more during the holiday season. But where does all this extra twinkle and shine come from? Well, Glitter Pixies, of course! And while I have never actually seen one with my own eyes, I find the evidence of where they have been everywhere in the place, and, yes, that even includes my face! In this project we're going to make piles of pixies perfect for putting on presents, crowning your cupcakes, or as ornaments twisted right onto your tree!

HERE'S EVERYTHING NEEDED FOR THIS MAKE AND DO! GATHER YOUR GLITTER, SCISSORS, AND GLUE.

Materials

- ½-inch-diameter wooden craft ball
- Toothpicks
- White glue
- Acrylic paints
- Light pink small chenille stems
- White small chenille stems
- Red small chenille stems
- Hot pink regular chenille stems
- Small craft box (optional)
- Glitter (optional)
- Satin ribbon (optional)

Tools

- Drill with 1⁄16-inch bit
- Toothpicks
- Wire cutters
- Ruler
- Paintbrushes
- Scissors
- Dowel
- Green Sharpie marker
- Red Sharpie marker

1 Make the head. Drill a hole approximately ¼ inch deep into the wooden craft ball. Insert a toothpick to temporarily hold the ball while you continue making the head.

2 Make the nose. Use wire cutters to cut approximately ¼ inch off of the end of a toothpick. Attach it to the face using white glue. Make the ears. Use wire cutters to snip the tip off of both ends of a toothpick. Use white glue to attach them to the sides of the head.

3 Base coat the head with flesh-colored acrylic paint. Add rosy pink cheeks. Allow to dry.

4 Paint the face. Start by color blocking the eyes, cheeks, and mouth, then add the details with a small brush. Set aside to dry.

5 Make the hat. Use scissors or wire cutters to cut a 6-inch piece of light pink small chenille stem. Wrap it around the top of a glue bottle or something similarly shaped, as shown. Slide it off and finish shaping it with your fingers.

6 Apply a few drops of white glue to the inside back of the hat and attach it to the head. This will prevent glue running down onto the face. Make the beard. Use scissors or wire cutters to cut a piece of a white small chenille stem that reaches from one side of the face to the other, and bend it into a U shape, as shown. Use white glue to attach it. Repeat with a second piece, attaching it just below the first.

6

7

8

7 Remove the temporary toothpick and place the head on a full-length 12-inch white small chenille stem. Secure it with white glue. Make the body. Use scissors or wire cutters to cut a 6-inch piece of red small chenille stem. Wrap it around a dowel or pencil to form a spiral, then gently slip it off. Slide the body up the long chenille stem, wrapping its end just under the beard to secure it.

8 Make the arms and hands. Use scissors or wire cutters to cut a 3¼-inch piece of white small chenille stem and bend approximately ⅛ inch at each end, as shown. Use a green Sharpie marker to color the center portion. This allows you to have two different colors on one stem of chenille.

9 Before closing the hands completely, use scissors or wire cutters to cut a 1-inch piece of white small chenille stem, shape it to look like a candy cane, and place it in one hand. Fold both hands shut. Push the arms between the coils of the body, as shown. Use a red Sharpie marker to add stripes to the candy cane.

10 Make the legs. Use scissors or wire cutters to cut a 5-inch piece of hot pink regular chenille stem. Fold it in half. Twist the top to make a loop and bend to look like legs and feet, as shown.

9

10

11 Push the loop at the top of the legs into the coiled body. Trim the fiber of the chenille stem with a small pair of scissors to give shape to the legs and feet.

12 Make a gift box. For small gifts, I like to use a craft box that I stripe and polka-dot using acrylic paints.

13 Brush the box with white glue and sprinkle with glitter. Allow to dry.

14 Tie on a satin ribbon bow. Use scissors to trim the stem of the pixie, as needed, and attach it to the package. Use your Glitter Pixie as a package trim or twist directly onto your tree.

Jolly Dolly Holly Wreath

There is nothing more enticing
than a wreath upon the door.
It welcomes all the passersby,
which is exactly what it's for!

For anyone who rings your bell,
or when the postman brings your mail,
or if a salesman comes to sell,
it's there to greet them without fail.

It's really such a simple thing,
a circlet made with something green.
It could be made from stringy beans,
but, I admit, that's something I've not seen.

Sometimes they're whipped up
from a neighbor's boxwood hedge,
that I climbed to get,
for the last time—I pledge!

I have always preferred mine
to be made of holly,
so it seems very tasteful,
but not overly jolly!

I do not suggest the normal kind.
You should get the rarest you can find,
made from holly grown at the North Pole,
with berries as pink as a pig, I'm told.

If Santa's holly you can't obtain,
then beget your own—let me explain!
Just grab some pom-poms and a bundle of felt,
copy the patterns, and make it yourself!

When it is all finished,
and people ask what it's for,
tell them it's a present,
especially for your front door!

1

2

Gather your glitter, scissors, and glue. Here's everything needed for this make and do!

Materials

- Wreath Pattern (page 177)
- Card stock
- 1 yard teal felt
- 1 yard lime green felt
- 1 yard turquoise felt
- Fiberfill
- Holly Leaf Pattern (page 177)
- Hot pink pom-poms, ½-inch diameter
- Red pom-poms, ½-inch diameter

Tools

- Photocopier
- Scissors
- Fabric marker
- Straight pins
- Sewing machine (optional)
- Ruler
- Kitchen skewer
- Needle and thread
- Iron and ironing board

Jolly Dolly Holly Wreath

If you're crafty and have a pet, then you probably know about their willingness to help you with anything you currently have spread out on a table. This was certainly the case with my pet chicken and this wreath project! From the time I laid out my felt and started cutting leaves, she was right in the middle of it all, carrying scraps and pushing pom-poms with her beak. So, instead of hanging my finished wreath on the door, it has become a holiday-themed nest for Miss Dolly Poulet!

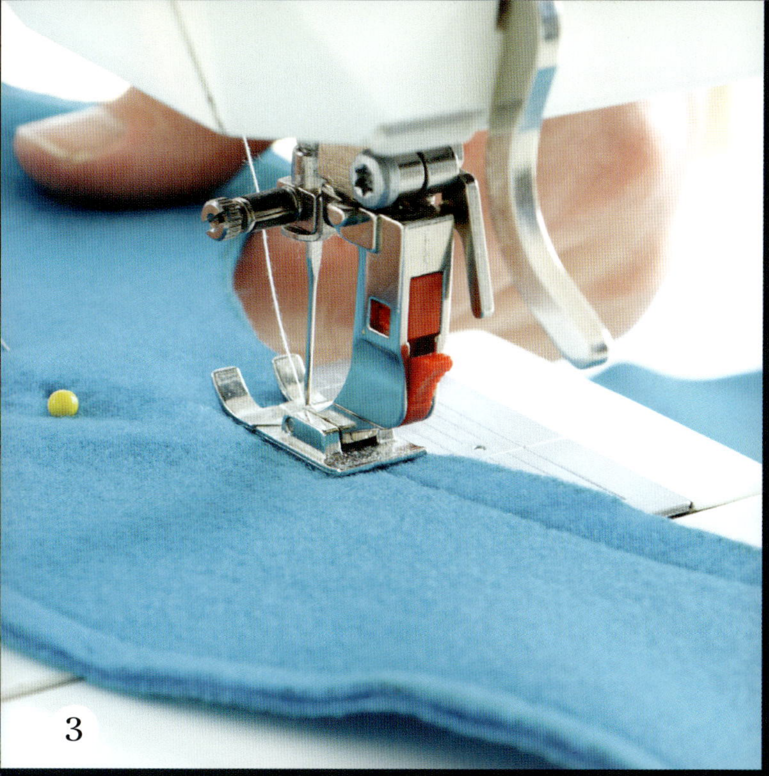

3

4

5

1 Make the wreath. Copy the Wreath Pattern on card stock and use scissors to cut it out. Place the pattern on a double layer of teal felt and trace around it with a fabric marker. Use scissors to cut out the wreath.

2 Pin the two pieces of felt together and use a sewing machine or needle and thread to sew a ¼-inch seam around the outer edge of the wreath. Leave approximately 2 inches open for adding fiberfill.

3 Sew around the inside edge of the wreath with a ¼-inch seam.

4 Stuff the wreath with fiberfill until it feels full and firm. Use a kitchen skewer to help get the stuffing all the way around.

5 Hand stitch the opening shut and set the wreath aside.

6 Make the holly leaves. Copy the Holly Leaf Pattern on card stock and use scissors to cut it out. Trace an equal number of holly leaves onto lime green and turquoise felt and use scissors to cut them out.

7 Stack a turquoise leaf on top of a lime green leaf and stitch down the center, to complete one holly leaf. Repeat this process for the remaining pieces. You will need approximately 129 holly leaves total.

8 To add dimension, separate the two leaves at the seam, as shown, and press open with an iron (low heat). Repeat this process for all of the remaining holly leaves.

9 Create clusters of three holly leaves by sewing them together at the tips with a needle and thread.

9

10

11

10 Once the three leaves are secure, thread two hot pink pom-poms and one red pom-pom onto the needle and slide them down to the holly leaf cluster.

11 Make a stitch through the holly leaf cluster to secure the pom-pom berries and finish by tying off the thread. Continue making clusters with berries for all of the remaining holly leaves.

12 Hand stitch the holly clusters to the front of the stuffed wreath form in a random pattern until the entire front of the wreath is covered. If desired, you can also add a felt ribbon by cutting a 1-inch-wide strip of felt and tacking it down throughout the holly with a needle and thread. Make the hanger. Use scissors to cut a 6- × 1-inch strip of lime green felt. Fold it in half and hand stitch it to the back of the wreath for hanging.

12

Glittered Baubles

Deep in the ground there's a Christmas mine,
where rare and sparkling jewels you'll find!

Only Santa's elves are allowed to go
to this magical place down beneath the snow.

They dig for glitter with shovels and picks,
and mark the spot with candy sticks.

This sparkly stuff is the telltale sign
of the brilliant gems they're about to find.

More precious than diamonds that are set into rings
are these bright baguettes that to the surface they bring.

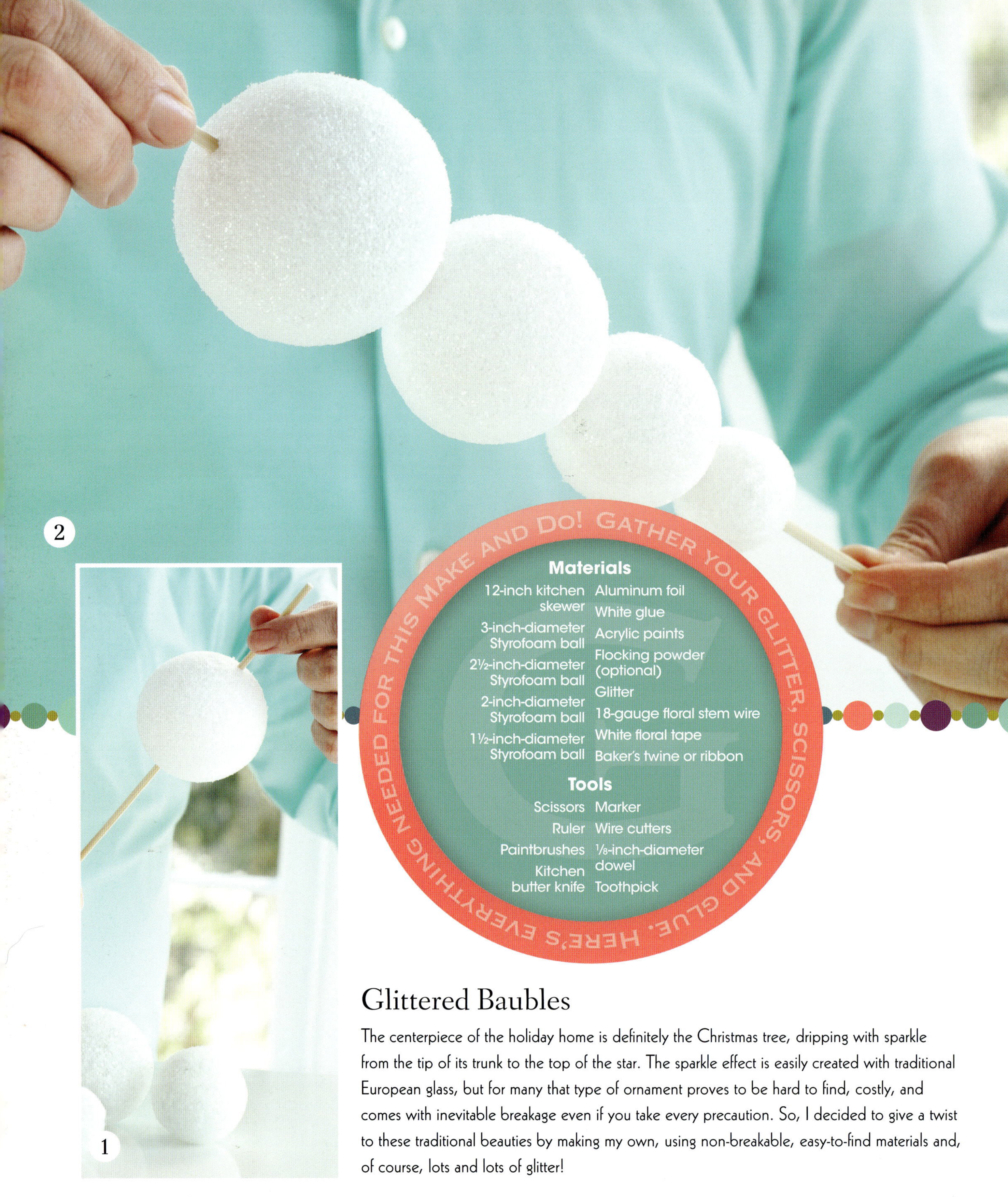

GATHER YOUR GLITTER, SCISSORS, AND GLUE. HERE'S EVERYTHING NEEDED FOR THIS MAKE AND DO!

Materials

- 12-inch kitchen skewer
- 3-inch-diameter Styrofoam ball
- 2½-inch-diameter Styrofoam ball
- 2-inch-diameter Styrofoam ball
- 1½-inch-diameter Styrofoam ball
- Aluminum foil
- White glue
- Acrylic paints
- Flocking powder (optional)
- Glitter
- 18-gauge floral stem wire
- White floral tape
- Baker's twine or ribbon

Tools

- Scissors
- Ruler
- Paintbrushes
- Kitchen butter knife
- Marker
- Wire cutters
- ⅛-inch-diameter dowel
- Toothpick

Glittered Baubles

The centerpiece of the holiday home is definitely the Christmas tree, dripping with sparkle from the tip of its trunk to the top of the star. The sparkle effect is easily created with traditional European glass, but for many that type of ornament proves to be hard to find, costly, and comes with inevitable breakage even if you take every precaution. So, I decided to give a twist to these traditional beauties by making my own, using non-breakable, easy-to-find materials and, of course, lots and lots of glitter!

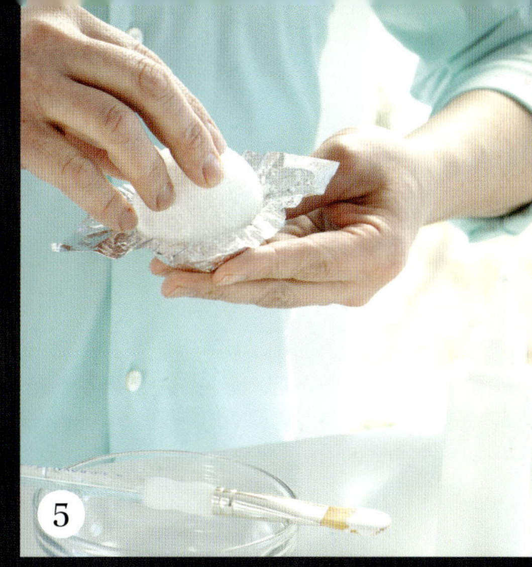

1 Make the ornament. Thread the 3-inch Styrofoam ball onto the kitchen skewer, making sure to keep the ball centered.

2 Repeat with the 2½-inch, 2-inch, and 1½-inch balls, sliding each one up to meet the next. This will be the shape of your ornament. Slide the balls off the skewer and set them aside in the same order.

3 To create a nice clean surface for painting and glittering, cover each ball in a layer of aluminum foil. Begin by cutting two 9 × 9-inch squares of aluminum foil for covering the 3-inch ball, two 7½ × 7½-inch squares for the 2½-inch ball, two 6 × 6-inch squares for the 2-inch ball, and two 4½ × 4½-inch squares for the 1½-inch ball.

4 Brush one half of the 3-inch ball with white glue.

5 Position the ball with the hole in the center of one of the foil squares.

6 Press the foil evenly over the glued half of the ball, leaving just the edges free.

7 Brush the other half of the ball with white glue and apply the second square of foil in the same way.

8 Use scissors to trim off excess foil around the ball, leaving approximately ⅛-inch allowance as shown. Brush the allowance with white glue and gently press down one side at a time.

9

10

11

12

13

14

9 Cover all the remaining balls using the same process. Slide them back onto the kitchen skewer in their previous order, using the same holes. Leave a small gap between each ball to provide space for painting and glittering. To create the patterns on each ball, gently press in the lines of the stripes using the blunt edge of a kitchen butter knife, and create the polka dots using the cap from a marker. Be careful not to tear the foil. If you do make a small tear in the foil, press it back down and secure it with white glue.

10 Using your patterned indentations as a guide, brush on the stripes and polka dots with acrylic paints. Allow to dry.

11 Brush with white glue and add flocking to desired areas. This step is optional and you can move straight to the next step if you prefer to use only glitter. I used flocking on the red stripe to give it additional depth. To make the ornament sparkle, brush each section with a light coat of white glue and sprinkle with colored glitter. You could also brush the entire ball with white glue and sprinkle uniformly with translucent iridescent glitter for an all-over sparkle.

12 When completely dry, push the balls together so the skewer is not visible between them. Use wire cutters to snip off any visible skewer from the top and bottom. Apply a dot of white glue to each end of the skewer and sprinkle with glitter to cover.

13 Make the hanger. Cut a 4-inch length of 18-gauge floral stem wire and wrap it with white floral tape. Bend the center of the wrapped wire around a ⅛-inch-diameter dowel to create a loop. Leave approximately 1 inch at each end, as shown.

14 Use a toothpick to make two small holes in the top of the ornament. Dip the ends of the hanger in white glue and insert into the two holes.

15 Add baker's twine or ribbon for hanging.

15

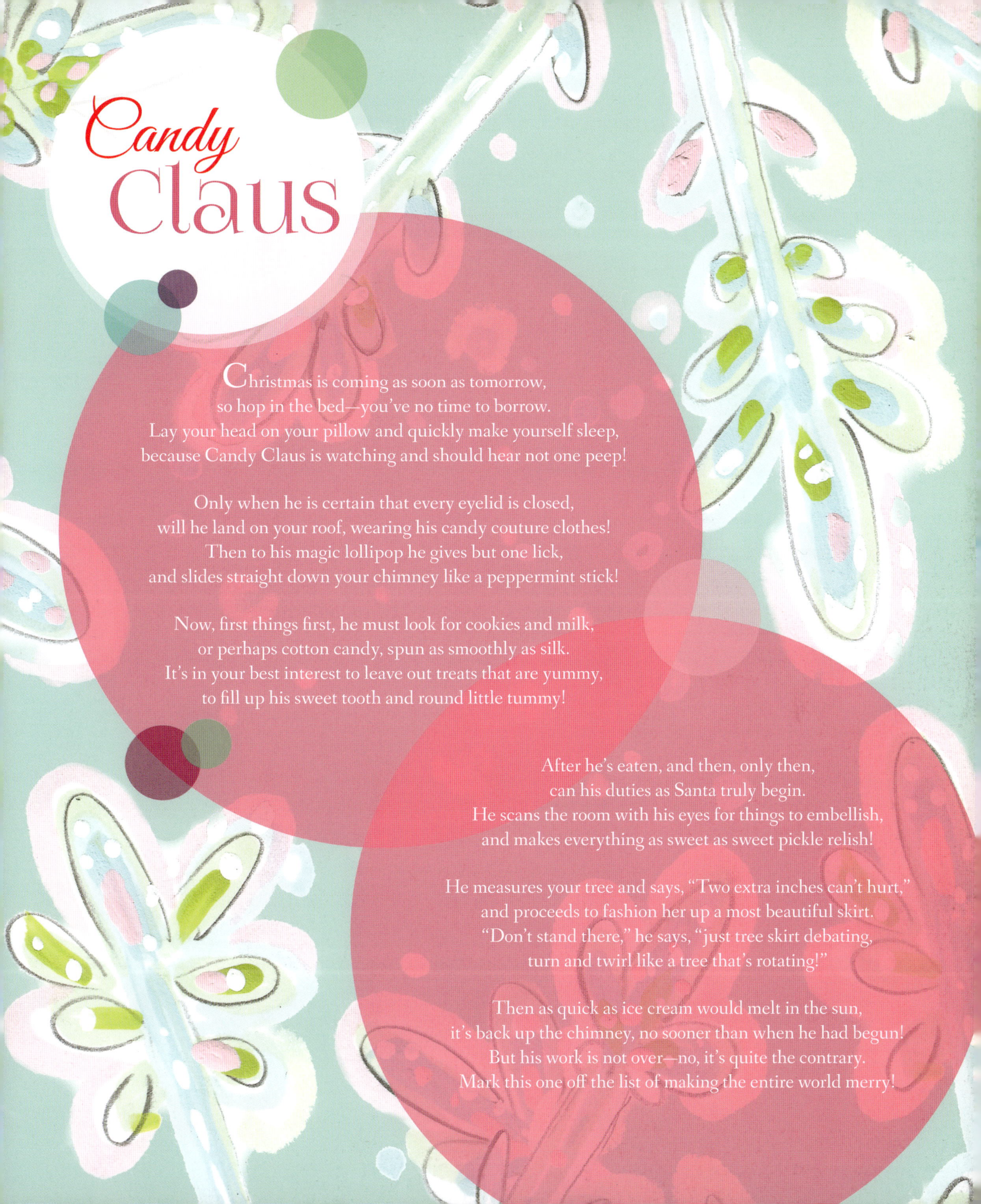

Candy Claus

Christmas is coming as soon as tomorrow,
so hop in the bed—you've no time to borrow.
Lay your head on your pillow and quickly make yourself sleep,
because Candy Claus is watching and should hear not one peep!

Only when he is certain that every eyelid is closed,
will he land on your roof, wearing his candy couture clothes!
Then to his magic lollipop he gives but one lick,
and slides straight down your chimney like a peppermint stick!

Now, first things first, he must look for cookies and milk,
or perhaps cotton candy, spun as smoothly as silk.
It's in your best interest to leave out treats that are yummy,
to fill up his sweet tooth and round little tummy!

After he's eaten, and then, only then,
can his duties as Santa truly begin.
He scans the room with his eyes for things to embellish,
and makes everything as sweet as sweet pickle relish!

He measures your tree and says, "Two extra inches can't hurt,"
and proceeds to fashion her up a most beautiful skirt.
"Don't stand there," he says, "just tree skirt debating,
turn and twirl like a tree that's rotating!"

Then as quick as ice cream would melt in the sun,
it's back up the chimney, no sooner than when he had begun!
But his work is not over—no, it's quite the contrary.
Mark this one off the list of making the entire world merry!

Candy Claus

Of all the crafts that I do, making folk art figures is probably what I consider to be the most rewarding! It's so much fun bringing a little character to life right before my eyes on the craft table. And although this project is a little more technical than some of the others, it's not rocket science. The how-to steps show you everything you need to know, and once you've made this sweet Santa, you can use the same techniques for making all the other characters you can think up, not just for Christmas, but all year long!

HERE'S EVERYTHING NEEDED FOR THIS MAKE AND DO! GATHER YOUR GLITTER, SCISSORS, AND GLUE.

Materials

- 1-inch-diameter Styrofoam ball
- Paperclay
- Two $\frac{1}{4}$-inch-diameter dowels
- Two 18-inch pieces of 16-gauge floral stem wire
- White floral tape
- Gesso
- Acrylic paints
- Fabrics for the coat, shirt, pants, and hat
- Coat Pattern (page 178) (optional)
- White glue
- White bump chenille stems
- White marabou
- Hat Pattern (page 178)
- Card stock
- $\frac{1}{2}$-inch-diameter white pom-pom
- Wooden craft base
- Sisal craft tree (available at craft stores) or Sparkle Forest tree (page 27)
- Gold leaf and gold leaf adhesive (optional)

Tools

- Pencil sharpener
- New #2 pencil with eraser
- Clay-sculpting tool
- Kitchen skewer (optional)
- Ruler
- Easy Cutter tool or hacksaw
- Pencil
- Drill with $\frac{1}{16}$-inch and $\frac{3}{32}$-inch bits
- Paintbrushes
- Fine-grade sandpaper (220 grit)
- Scissors
- Photocopier
- Wire cutters
- Fabric marker
- Needle and thread
- Hot glue gun

1 Make the head. Dip the Styrofoam ball in water to moisten it, then place it in the center of a flattened circle of Paperclay.

2 Pull the Paperclay up around the ball. Work the air bubbles up and out of the opening before squeezing the clay shut.

3 Roll the ball between your hands until even and smooth.

4 Push the ball onto a sharpened ¼-inch-diameter dowel. Be careful not to push all the way through. The dowel will help you hold the head while you are working on it. With your finger, gently make indentations in the clay for the eyes.

5 Moisten the backs of two round balls of Paperclay and attach them to the face to create cheeks, as shown.

6 Add a small ball of Paperclay for the nose. Smooth and add detail with a clay-sculpting tool.

7 Make two small rolls of Paperclay for the mustache. Shape with your fingers and curl the ends. Moisten the Paperclay and attach the mustache to the face.

8 Use a sculpting tool or the end of a kitchen skewer to make the mouth. Set the head aside and allow the Paperclay to harden.

9 Make the body. Cut a dowel approximately 3 inches long for the torso. You can use an Easy Cutter tool, but a hacksaw will work just fine.

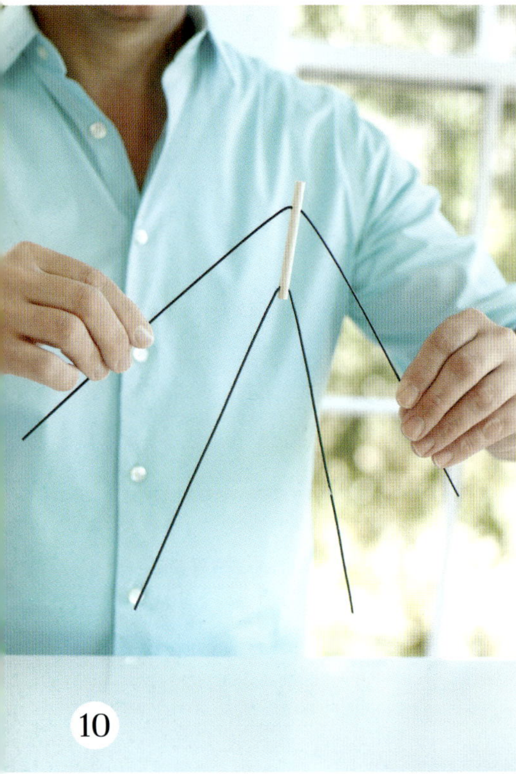

10 Use a pencil to mark the placement of the arms and legs. Leave enough room at the neck end for attaching the head. Use a drill with a 1⁄16-inch bit to drill holes all the way through the dowel at each of the places you marked. Insert one 18-inch piece of 16-gauge floral stem wire through each of the two holes. Bend the wires down, as shown.

11 Keep the wires in place by wrapping them with floral tape. Wrap the dowel, arms, and legs with floral tape.

12 Cover the dowel with Paperclay and continue adding layers to build up the torso. You will need to let each layer partially dry before adding the next.

13 Shape and blend until you have formed the body. Allow the Paperclay to harden completely.

14 Coat the entire figure with gesso to fill in any imperfections and allow to dry completely. Sand the figure lightly with fine-grade sandpaper until smooth. If gesso is not available, just apply multiple coats of white paint and sand until smooth.

15 Even though the body will be covered by fabric later, paint on the clothes with acrylic paints so that no white shows through a seam or weave in the fabric.

16 Paint the legs and arms and allow to dry, then add stripes. Set aside to dry.

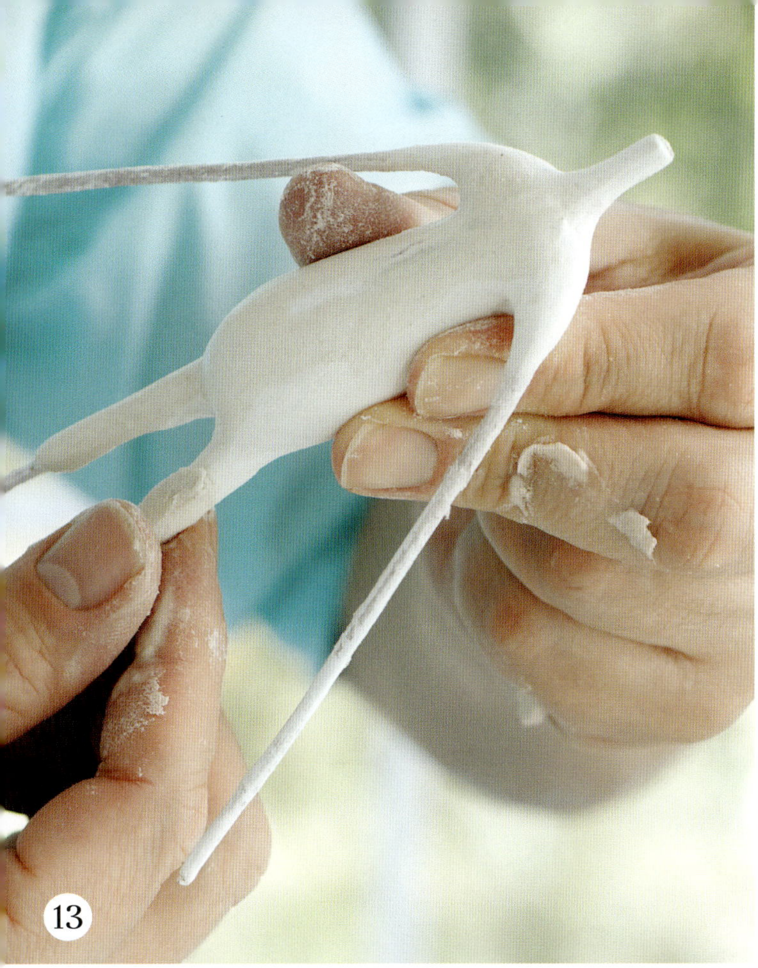

13

14

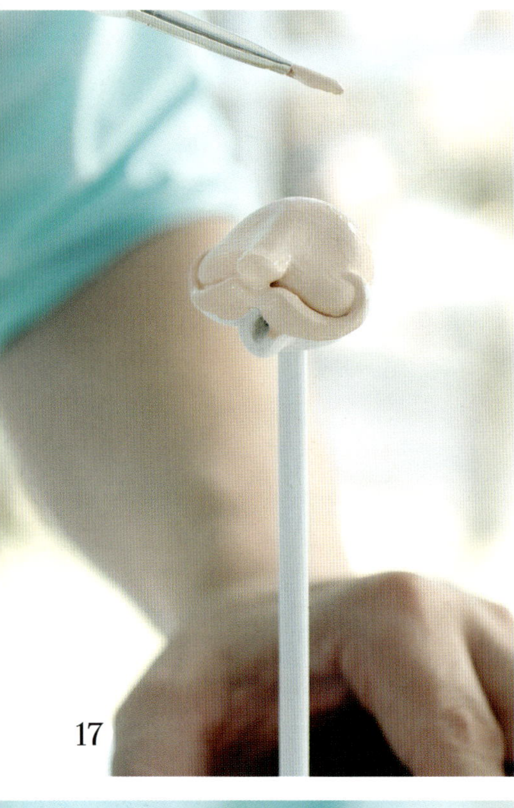
17

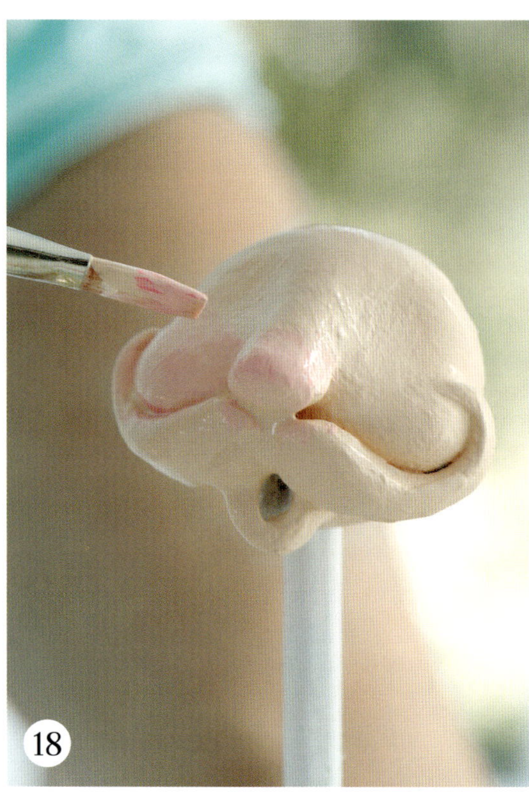
18

19

20

17 Paint a flesh-colored base coat on the head and allow to dry.

18 Paint the nose and cheeks with pink acrylic to add blush.

19 Use acrylic paints to color block the eyes, mustache, and mouth.

20 Finish the details of the face.

21 Bend the arms into position.

22 Make the clothes. Brush the back of the torso with white glue.

23 Lay a small piece of fabric onto the back and use your finger to press into the glue.

24 Use scissors to trim up the sides of the body and under the arms.

25 Repeat the steps on the front of the torso, being sure to match the fabrics at the shoulder and side seams.

21
22
23
24
25

26

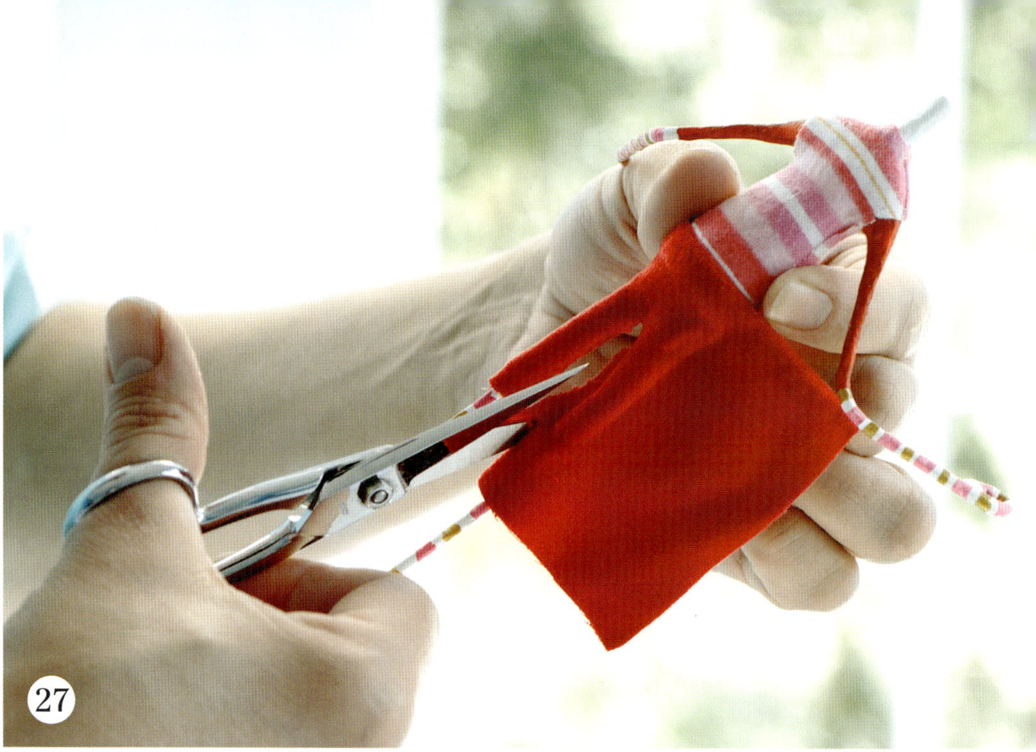

27

28

29

30

31

26 For the pants, cut a piece of fabric approximately 3 inches wide by 3½ inches long. Turn over the edge of the longer side and secure with a few drops of white glue.

27 Using the same technique as before, brush the back of the pants with white glue, position the fabric with the turned edge at the waist band, and press the fabric into the glue with your fingers. Trim the excess fabric at the side seam. Repeat on the front.

28 Brush the arms with white glue and use the same techniques from above to create the sleeves.

29 Make the coat. Use the Coat Pattern to cut the coat out of fabric. Cut slits where indicated on the pattern for the arms. Adjust the size as needed for your specific figure.

30 Pin the two coat pieces onto contrasting fabric, wrong sides together, and cut out using scissors.

31 Glue the pieces together with white glue as shown, being careful not to use too much. Set aside to dry.

32 Make the boots. Wrap rectangular pieces of Paperclay around the bottom of the legs and close the opening with a moistened finger. Add small rectangles of clay around the top of each boot to make cuffs. Add pieces of clay to make the toe and heel of the boot, leaving enough wire exposed at the bottom to attach Santa to the base. Set aside and allow the Paperclay to harden.

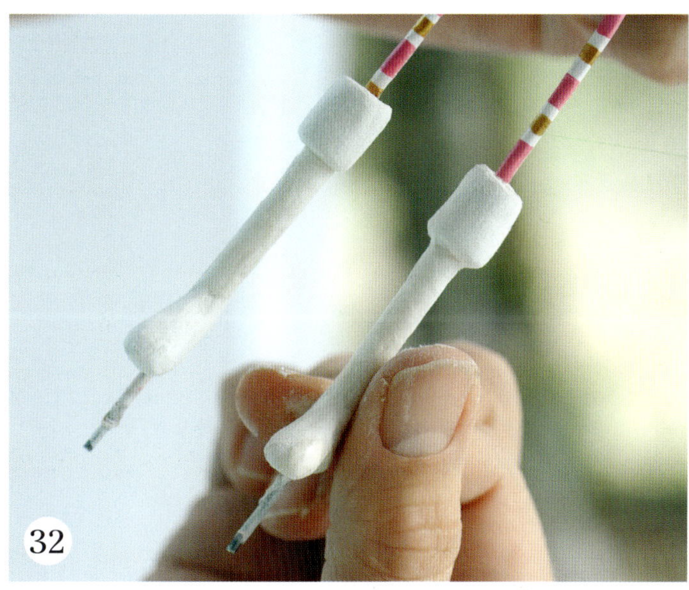

32

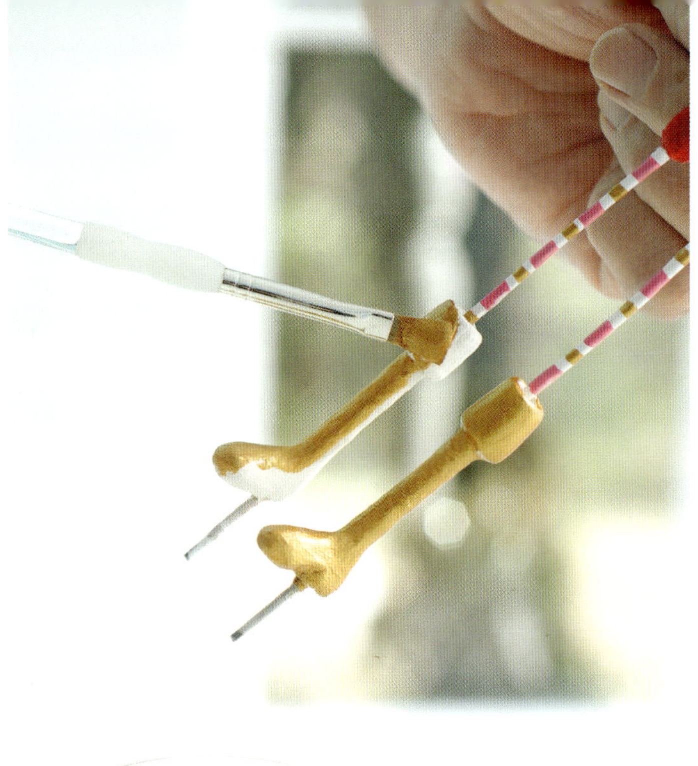

33

34

35

33 Paint the boots with gold acrylic.

34 Brush the boots with gold leaf adhesive and apply the gold leaf (optional).

35 Make the hands. Attach small pieces of Paperclay to create the hands. Shape one hand to look like it is grasping a skinny Christmas tree. Allow the Paperclay to harden, then paint and allow to dry.

36 Cut two identical, thick strips of the striped shirt fabric to trim the bottom of the coat. Press the strips in half lengthwise with an iron. Sandwich the bottom edge of each coat piece between the front and back of its trim and secure with white glue as shown. Use white glue to attach the trim to both the inside and outside of each coat piece. Cut ends of trim to fit.

37 Slide the coat pieces onto each arm. Roll the front edges back to create a collar and lapel.

38 Stitch the back closed with a hand needle and thread.

36
37
38

39 Attach the head with white glue, then apply a circle of marabou with hot glue to create Santa's beard and hair.

40 Wrap the sleeve and pant ends with small pieces of bump chenille to make fuzzy cuffs.

41 Make the base. Cover a plain wooden base with Paperclay and shape into a mound of snow; add discs of clay to look like candies. Allow to dry.

42 Paint the base a snowy white with some subtle blue shading. Color block the candies and then add the details. Allow to dry.

43 Brush with white glue and sprinkle with glitter.

44 Drill two holes using a $\frac{3}{32}$-inch bit in the wooden craft base. Attach the figure by dipping the exposed wires below the boots in white glue and inserting them into the holes.

41

42

43

44

45

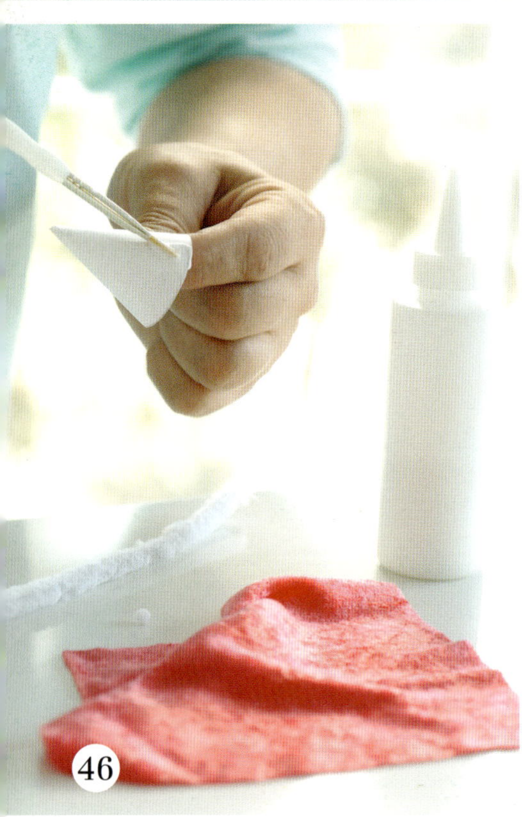
46

47

45 Attach Santa to the base by inserting the feet into the holes.

46 Make the hat. Copy the Hat Pattern on card stock and use scissors to cut it out. Roll into the shape and secure with white glue. Brush the cone with white glue and cover with fabric, cutting the excess at the back seam and bottom. Make a loop of white chenille and wrap around the bottom edge. Attach a small white pom-pom to the tip and fold the top of the hat over.

47 Attach the hat in the back with a few drops of hot glue.

48 Put a small sisal tree in Santa's hand with hot glue. To recolor a store-bought sisal tree, follow the techniques found in the Sparkle Forest project on page 27.

Cherry Christmas

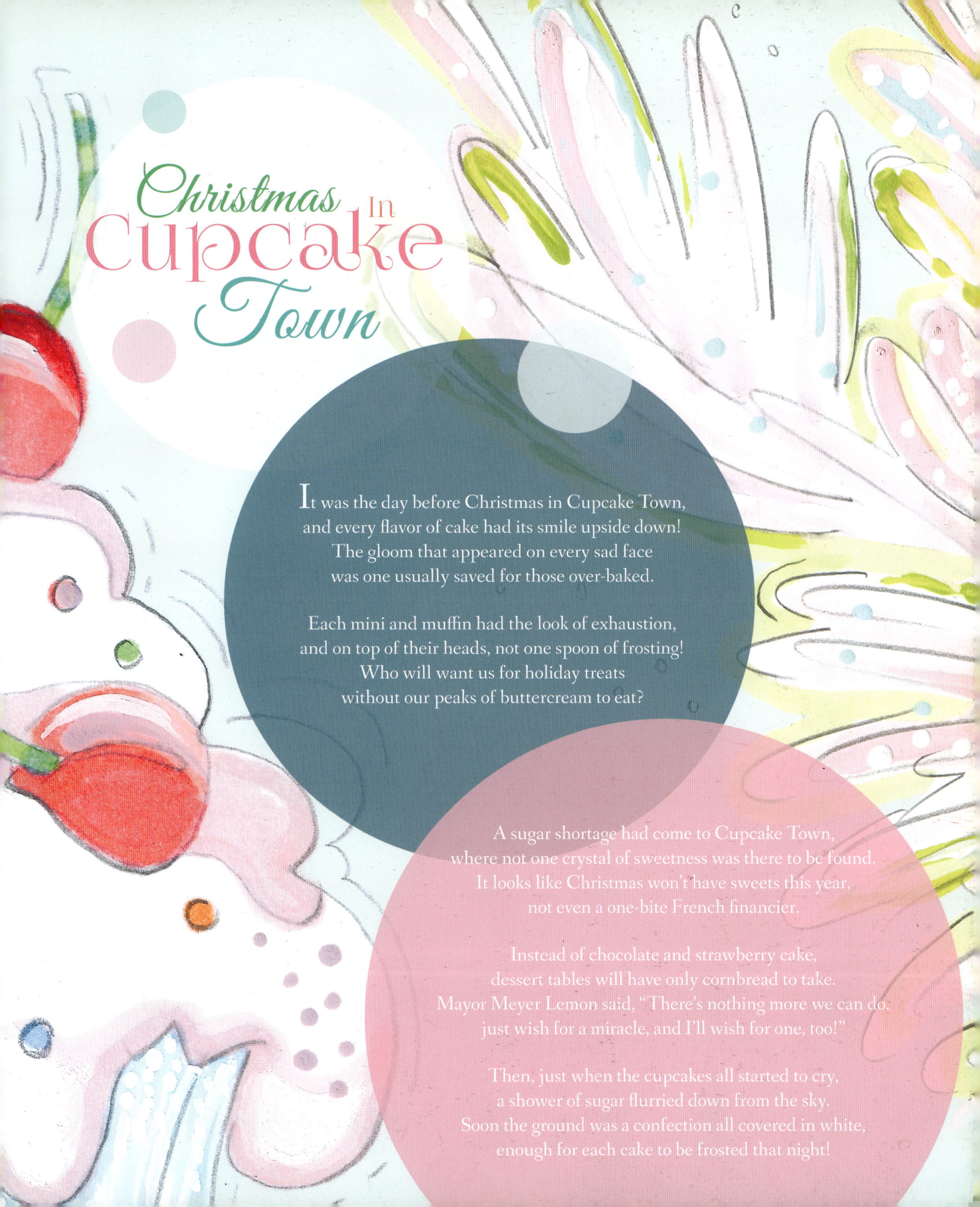

Christmas in Cupcake Town

It was the day before Christmas in Cupcake Town,
and every flavor of cake had its smile upside down!
The gloom that appeared on every sad face
was one usually saved for those over-baked.

Each mini and muffin had the look of exhaustion,
and on top of their heads, not one spoon of frosting!
Who will want us for holiday treats
without our peaks of buttercream to eat?

A sugar shortage had come to Cupcake Town,
where not one crystal of sweetness was there to be found.
It looks like Christmas won't have sweets this year,
not even a one-bite French financier.

Instead of chocolate and strawberry cake,
dessert tables will have only cornbread to take.
Mayor Meyer Lemon said, "There's nothing more we can do,
just wish for a miracle, and I'll wish for one, too!"

Then, just when the cupcakes all started to cry,
a shower of sugar flurried down from the sky.
Soon the ground was a confection all covered in white,
enough for each cake to be frosted that night!

Christmas in Cupcake Town

Almost anyone who knows me will tell you that Stephen Brown loves cupcakes, and I will have to say that it is true! I love that cupcakes wear pleated paper skirts, I love that they smell like butter, and I love how the icing piles up in a twirl on top like they have just come from getting their hair frosted. In fact, I see each cupcake as an individual, not just number thirteen in a baker's dozen, which is why I started giving my cupcakes faces and personalities as big as they are yummy!

GATHER YOUR GLITTER, SCISSORS, AND GLUE. HERE'S EVERYTHING NEEDED FOR THIS MAKE AND DO!

Materials

- 18-inch piece of 18-gauge floral stem wire
- White floral tape
- Acrylic paints
- 3- × 2-inch Styrofoam cone
- 2-inch-diameter Styrofoam ball
- Toothpicks
- Paperclay
- Heart Wire Template (page 179)
- Card stock
- White glue
- Red flocking powder
- Glitter
- 20-gauge floral stem wire
- Heart Pattern (page 179)
- Hot pink regular chenille stem
- Banner Art (page 179)
- Ribbon or baker's twine

Tools

- Paintbrushes
- Serrated knife
- Ruler
- Wire cutters
- New #2 pencil with eraser
- Clay-sculpting tool
- Needle-nose pliers
- Photocopier
- Fine-grade sandpaper (220 grit)
- Drill with 1/8-inch bit and 1/16-inch bit
- Scissors

1 Wrap the 18-inch piece of 18-gauge floral stem wire with white floral tape.

2 Paint the covered wire with a base coat and allow to dry. Add stripes with a small detail brush and set aside to dry.

3 Make the cupcake. With a serrated knife, cut approximately 1 inch from the top and ½ inch from the bottom of the Styrofoam cone. This will be the base of the cupcake. These measurements are pretty specific for the materials I'm using, but you can basically just cut a Styrofoam cone to be the size you want your cupcake to be.

4 Cut the 2-inch-diameter Styrofoam ball in half with the serrated knife. This will be the icing on your cupcake.

5 Place the frosting on top of the base as shown and push in toothpicks to hold them together.

6 Use wire cutters to trim the toothpicks to be even with the Styrofoam.

7 With the eraser end of a new #2 pencil, gently make indentations in the Styrofoam for the eyes.

8 Make a roll of Paperclay and flatten it into a rectangle. Apply this to the sides of the cupcake base and press into the indentations for the eyes. Smooth and blend with your fingers or clay-sculpting tool.

9 Create the mouth by pressing into the Paperclay with a clay-sculpting tool or your fingers.

10 Add balls of Paperclay to the top. Shape and smooth the Paperclay with your fingers to form the icing on the cupcake.

11 Attach and blend two small balls of Paperclay for the cheeks. Remember to moisten with water before adding, to ensure that they stick.

10

11

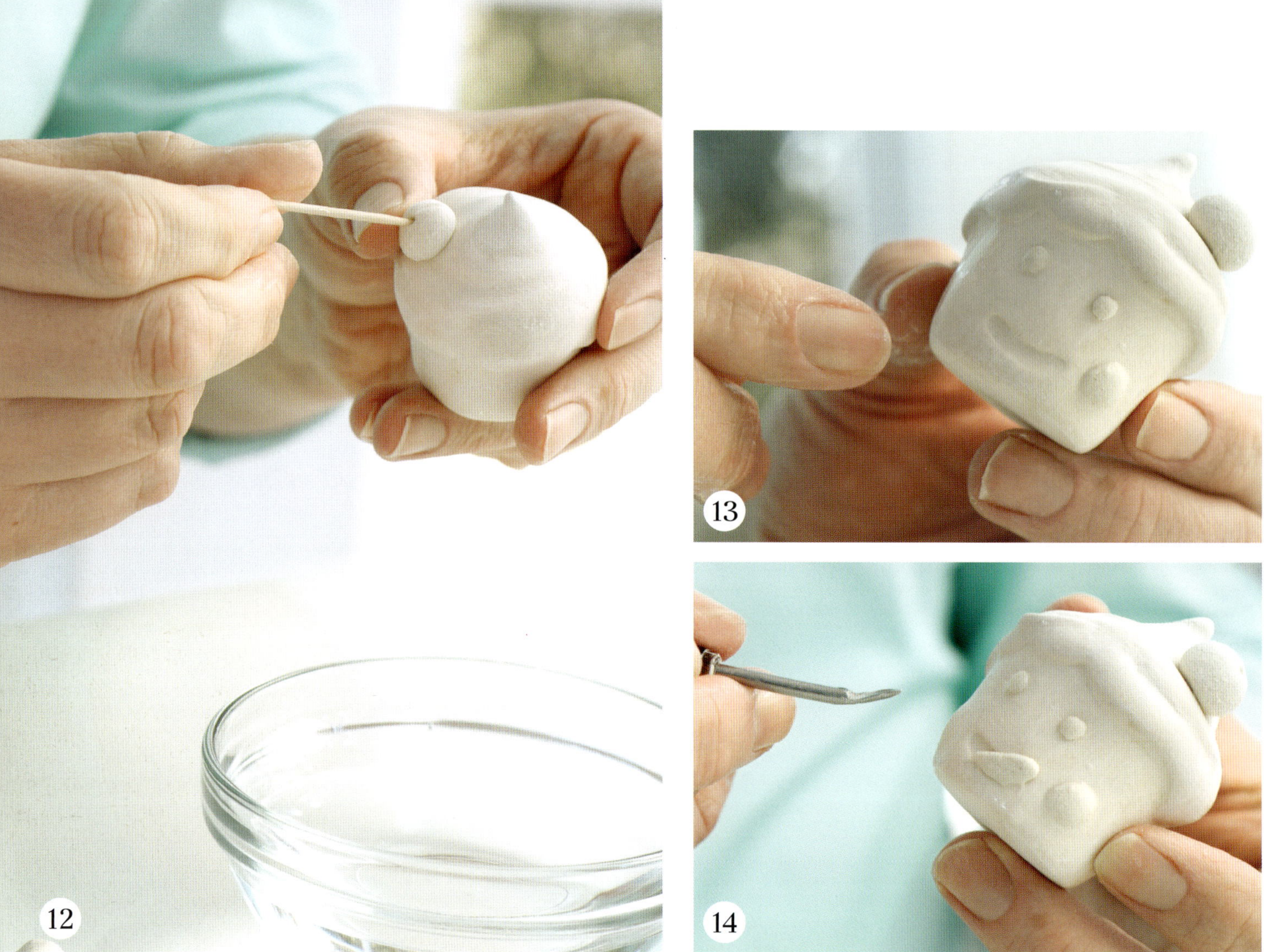

12 Make a cherry for the top of the cupcake from a ball of Paperclay. Use a toothpick to make a small hole in the top for inserting the stem later.

13 Add two small balls of Paperclay to the eye indentations for pupils.

14 Use a sculpting tool to shape a small piece of Paperclay into a tongue and attach it to the mouth. Set the cupcake aside and allow the Paperclay to harden.

15 Make the heart frame. Hold both ends of the striped wire and slowly bend them toward each other, creating an arch.

16 Cross the ends of the striped wire, reposition your hands, and continue bending until you create a small loop at the top as shown.

17 Flip the loop over and continue bringing the ends back together. You should see the heart shape starting to form. If needed, check your finished heart against the Wire Heart Template and make adjustments as necessary.

18 Use needle-nose pliers to bend ½ inch of the ends of the wire inward. Be careful not to overwork the wire.

15
16
17
18

19
20
21

19 Prepare the cupcake for painting by lightly sanding the surface with fine-grade sandpaper. Paint a base coat and then color block the cupcake and frosting, including the eyes and mouth. Allow to dry.

20 Use a small brush to paint the details of the face and allow to completely dry.

21 Make the sprinkles. Use wire cutters to cut toothpicks into small pieces. Attach them to the cupcake icing using white glue. Use a small brush to paint them and allow them to dry.

22 Brush the cherry with white glue and use your fingers to cover it with red flocking powder. Brush the frosting with white glue and sprinkle it with iridescent glitter. For the stem of the cherry, dip the end of a small piece of painted 20-gauge floral stem wire in white glue and insert it in the hole.

23 Use a drill with a 1/16-inch bit to make a hole, centered on each side of the cupcake, as shown. This is where the ends of the wire heart will be inserted. Just below each of these holes, use the tip of a craft knife to make a smaller hole for the chenille arms. Use the 1/16-inch drill bit to make one hole in the center of the bottom of the cupcake.

24 Dip the bent ends of the heart wire in white glue and insert them into the larger holes on the sides of the cupcake.

22

23

24

25 Copy the Heart Pattern on card stock and use scissors to cut out two hearts. Brush the back of each heart with white glue and sandwich a painted toothpick between them. Paint the heart pink and allow it to dry. Brush both sides of the heart with white glue and sprinkle with glitter.

26 Dip the end of the painted toothpick in white glue and insert it into the hole in the bottom of the cupcake.

27 Make the arms. Cut the chenille stem into two 3-inch pieces and bend the ends into a mitten shape. Dip the ends of the arms in white glue and insert them into the holes on the sides of the cupcake.

28 Copy the Banner Art on card stock and use scissors to cut it out. Use white glue to attach the front piece of the banner across the middle of the wire heart, as shown. Attach the back of the banner in the same way. Add a piece of ribbon or baker's twine for hanging.

26

27

28

Coconut Flake Cake

In my kitchen I am making
something scrumptious I'll be taking
to a party for which I'm baking
this masterpiece, without mistaking.

I will stir it up with flour and stuff,
a recipe I've come to trust,
and in the oven it will puff,
with egg whites to give it extra fluff!

Soon it's out and on a cooling rack,
with perfect tops, free of cracks.
I put away the sugar sacks
and think, "For baking, I have a knack!"

I cut the layers from thick to thin,
to hold the fillings I'll spread in.
People's taste buds I'm sure to win,
and be asked to make this cake again.

On the top, its frosting's plopped.
This masterpiece cannot be stopped,
and add to that, it can't be topped—
except with coconut freshly chopped.

Now it's ready to be eaten,
all mouths are full, no one is speaking.
There's nothing left—not one small crumb.
One word describes it, and that is, "YUM!"

Materials

- Styrofoam balls in various sizes (1-inch diameter up to 2½-inch diameter)
- Paperclay
- Gesso (optional)
- Acrylic paints
- Kitchen skewers
- Toothpicks
- White glue
- Glitter
- Regular chenille stems (optional)
- Card stock (optional)

Tools

- Felt-tip marker
- Fine-grade sandpaper (220 grit)
- Paintbrushes
- Pencil
- Wire cutters
- Drill with assorted-sized bits
- Colored pencils

Flakey Friends

I love baking outlandishly large layer cakes with creamy fillings and fluffy frosting. They are not only super-duper yummy; they make the perfect centerpiece for any and every holiday table. I have included a recipe that is one of my favorites, and it starts with a moist white cake that is filled with coconut lemon cream and perfectly peaked with piles of white seven-minute frosting. But before you preheat the oven, go to your craft table and get ready to make a few Flakey Friends to top off this spectacular creation!

1 To make each Flake, use a felt-tip marker to draw the eyes and mouth onto a 3-inch diameter Styrofoam ball. Make a small dot to indicate where the nose will go.

2 Use your thumbs or the end of a marker to make indentations for the eyes and mouth.

3 Dip the ball in water to slightly moisten it. This will make the Paperclay adhere better.

4 Cover the ball with flattened pieces of Paperclay.

5 Smooth and blend the Paperclay until the ball is evenly covered.

6 Make the frosting. Roll out a piece of Paperclay approximately 6 inches long. Coil it on top of the ball, as shown. Moisten your fingers and use them to smooth and blend the dollop of frosting.

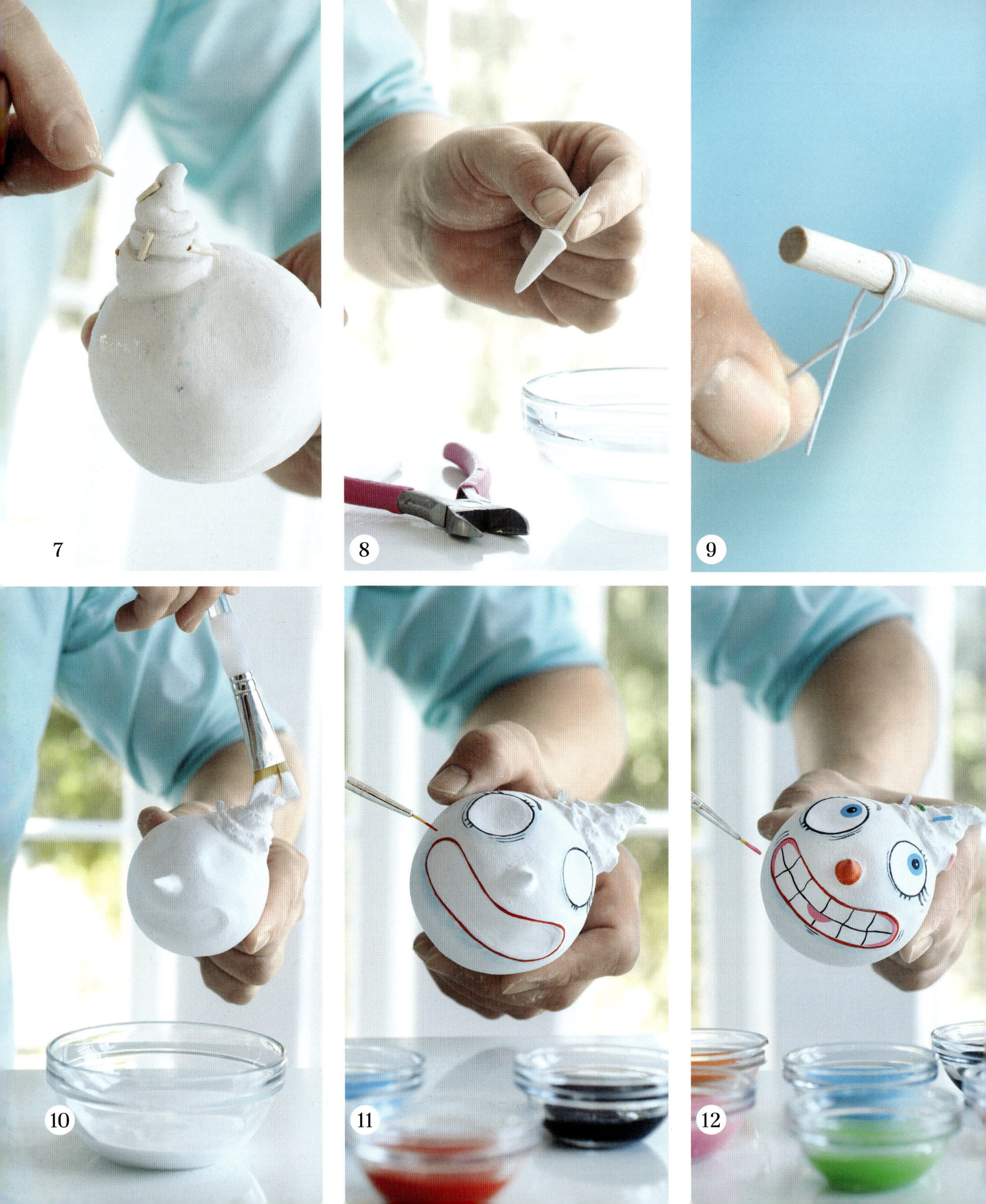
7
8
9
10
11
12

13

7 Make the sprinkles. Use wire cutters to cut toothpicks into small pieces. Press the sprinkles into the frosting.

8 Make the nose. Use wire cutters to cut the pointed end of a kitchen skewer to a length of approximately 2 inches. Cover the cut end of the skewer with Paperclay and use your fingers to shape and smooth it. Gently push the pointed end of the skewer into the face and blend the nose with your fingers.

9 Make the hanger. Wrap a piece of floral stem wire approximately 4 inches around a kitchen skewer to shape it, as shown. Remove the hanger from the skewer and gently push the ends into the top of the Flake, behind the frosting. Allow the Paperclay to harden.

10 Sand the Flake lightly with fine-grade sandpaper. Brush the entire Flake with a coat of gesso or white acrylic paint and allow to dry.

11 Use a round brush to add light blue shading around the eyes, nose, and mouth. Use a pencil to lightly sketch the features of the face. Use a fine paintbrush to outline the eyes and mouth.

12 Paint the details of the face and nose.

13 Brush the head with white glue and sprinkle with glitter. To add extra sparkle, apply gold leaf to the nose.

14 Use your imagination to finish off your Flake with accessories made from chenille stems and card stock (party hats) as shown on page 128, or leave them as sparkling snowballs!

Coconut Cake

Now you're ready to start baking the cake! Although I have included my recipe for a delicious white cake to make from scratch, you could also choose to use your own favorite recipe, or even a cake mix to achieve similar results. The grandeur of this cake is the total sum of its parts and, frankly, even a mediocre cake can be saved by the fillings and frostings . . . so do not fear! That said, if you choose to use a cake mix (which is not against the laws of baking), there are basic preparation tips that can help you make a boxed mix taste like it's made from scratch. First, you should always sift the boxed dry ingredients through a wire strainer to remove all the lumps. After the batter is mixed as directed on the box, it's very important to add additional flavorings to give the cake a more distinct flavor. My preference is to always add between 1 and 2 tablespoons of real vanilla extract and a dash of fresh lemon juice. You can also add a small amount of almond flavoring but with measured caution, as it can quickly take over the flavor. So, make your baking plan and get started!

1 Make the cake. Preheat the oven to 350°F. Grease two 8-inch round cake pans with unsalted butter. Cut two 8-inch circles of parchment paper. Place one in the bottom of each pan and dust with flour.

2 Combine the milk, egg whites, and vanilla in a medium-sized bowl and blend with a fork. Set aside.

3 Mix the cake flour, sugar, baking powder, and salt in the bowl of an electric mixer on low speed. Add the butter and beat until the mixture is the texture of moist crumbs.

4 Add half of the milk mixture to the butter mixture and beat on medium speed for 1½ minutes. Add the remaining half of the milk mixture and beat for 1 minute more.

5 Use a spatula to divide the batter between the two prepared pans. Bake until golden and a toothpick inserted in the center comes out clean, 25 to 30 minutes.

6 Remove the cakes from the pans and transfer to wire racks to cool completely before filling and frosting.

Make and Do! Gather your glitter, scissors, and glue. Here's everything needed for this

Ingredients

1 (16-ounce) container sour cream

1 cup sugar

Juice of 2 lemons

2 tablespoons vanilla extract

Tools

Medium-sized bowl

Spatula

Lemon Filling

The filling can be made in advance and refrigerated for a few days, until ready to use.

1 Make the filling. Combine the sour cream and sugar in a medium-sized bowl and stir until the sugar is dissolved and no longer grainy.

2 Add the lemon juice and vanilla and stir until thoroughly combined.

Fluffy White Frosting

1 Make the frosting. Combine the egg whites, sugar, water, corn syrup, and salt in the top of a double boiler and place it over boiling water.

2 On the highest speed of an electric mixer, beat constantly for 6 to 8 minutes, until the frosting forms soft peaks.

3 Remove from the heat, add the vanilla, and beat for 1 minute more.

HERE'S EVERYTHING NEEDED FOR THIS MAKE AND DO! GATHER YOUR GLITTER, SCISSORS, AND GLUE.

Ingredients

3 large egg whites
2¼ cups sugar
½ cup cold water
1½ tablespoons light corn syrup
⅛ teaspoon salt
1½ teaspoons vanilla extract

Tools

Double boiler
Electric mixer

1

2

GATHER YOUR GLITTER, SCISSORS, AND GLUE. HERE'S EVERYTHING NEEDED FOR THIS MAKE AND DO!

Ingredients

28 ounces sweetened flaked coconut (approximate amount)

Silver dragées, colorful nonpareils, gumballs, and other cake decorations (optional)

Tools

Long serrated knife

Serving plate

Offset spatula

Assembling the Cake

1 Slice each cake layer in half using a long serrated knife.

2 Place the first layer on a plate, cut side up, and spread the top with filling, then add a thin layer of coconut. Repeat with the remaining layers until you reach the top layer, placing it on top with the cut side down.

3 Put a large dollop of frosting on top of the cake and spread it down the sides. Continue until the entire cake is covered.

4 Cover the top and sides with coconut and decorate with the Flakey Friends. Add dragées or other decorations as desired.

3
4

Pink Chenille Pine With Sappy Sweet Ornaments

I thought that I would never find
a perfectly shaped pink Christmas pine.

Now, some say, or demand, that a tree must be green,
but they say this because it's all they have seen!

I prefer decoration that's not the obvious colors,
like yellow—not bright, but subtle like butter.

Why does everything in the world have to be always the same?
In my opinion, that's as dull as if we all had the same name!

If we were all called Harry, I'd hate that, I think . . .
as much as the idea that Christmas trees can't be pink!

HERE'S EVERYTHING NEEDED FOR THIS MAKE AND DO! GATHER YOUR GLITTER, SCISSORS, AND GLUE.

Materials

Wood finial, approximately 4½ inches tall
Gesso (optional)
Acrylic paints
3- × 6-inch Styrofoam cone
White glue
Kitchen skewer
Hot pink regular chenille stems
Light pink regular chenille stems

Tools

Paintbrushes
Ruler
Wire cutters
Hot glue gun

Pink Chenille Pine with Sappy Sweet Ornaments

Won't Santa be surprised when he goes looking for those cookies you left out for him, but finds this fabulous pink tree trimmed with candies and cookies of every kind instead! The tree is easily made by pushing lengths of chenille stems into Styrofoam, and is a great project for all ages. But the real fun is making all of the miniature ornaments and decorating it just like you would a real tree.

1

2

1 Prepare the base. Coat the finial with gesso or white acrylic paint and allow to dry completely.

2 Paint the finial and add details. Allow to dry completely.

3 Push the top of the wooden finial approximately 1½ inches deep into the bottom of the Styrofoam cone or until the finial seems secure enough to hold the tree. Then, remove the finial from the cone.

4 Fill the cavity of the Styrofoam cone with white glue and reinsert the finial. Make sure to wipe away any excess glue that drips out. Allow the glue to dry completely.

4

3

5 Make the tree. Measure 5½ inches from the pointed end of a kitchen skewer and use wire cutters to cut off the excess. Dip the end of the skewer in white glue and insert it into the top of the cone approximately 1 inch deep. Allow the glue to dry.

6 Take one hot pink chenille stem and wrap approximately 2 inches of its length around the top of the skewer, as shown. Slide the chenille up enough on the skewer to allow you to add a drop of hot glue, then move the chenille back into place.

7 Measure 6 inches up the chenille stem and fold it back on itself at this point.

8 Wrap the folded piece of the chenille stem around the other half to make one stem, as shown. This completes the frame of the tree.

9 The branches of the tree are made from a series of hot and light pink chenille stems that are cut into pieces, ranging from 1½ inches to 3¾ inches long. You will start by adding the branches at the bottom. Use wire cutters to cut twenty-five chenille stems of each color into 2-inch pieces. This number is approximate. Depending on your spacing, you can use many more or less. Begin inserting the chenille branches around the bottom of the cone about ¼ inch into the cone. Continue this process until you have covered approximately 4 inches up the cone. The idea is to insert enough branches to make a full tree, but not so many that you break down the structure of the Styrofoam.

7
8
9

13

10 Use wire cutters to cut additional chenille stems of both colors into 1½-inch pieces and continue covering the remaining portion of the Styrofoam cone. The tree should begin to take shape.

11 At this point, you are ready to start adding branches to the skewer. Cut both colors of chenille stems into 3¾-inch pieces. Wrap them around the skewer as shown, continuing halfway up the skewer. I used approximately 5 stems of each color, but you may use more or less.

12 Cover the remainder of the skewer with 3-inch pieces of both colors wrapped in the same way.

13 To finish off the branches of the tree, continue with the same wrapping method. Start with 3-inch pieces followed by 2½-inch , 1¾-inch, and finally 1½-inch pieces as you reach the top.

14 Create the swirl at the top of the tree by bending the chenille branches into shape with your fingers.

GATHER YOUR GLITTER, SCISSORS, AND GLUE. HERE'S EVERYTHING NEEDED FOR THIS MAKE AND DO!

Materials

- Small chenille stems
- Beads in various sizes and shapes
- Jewelry pins
- Acrylic paints
- Glitter
- Paperclay
- White glue
- Toothpicks
- 32-gauge jewelry wire
- Star-shaped bead (optional)

Tools

- Wire cutters
- Round-nose pliers
- Paintbrushes
- Craft knife

Sappy Sweet Ornaments

Cookies and Candies

Roll out a thin layer of Paperclay. Cut out shapes with a craft knife and allow them to harden. Paint the cookies and cakes with acrylic paints and allow them to dry. Don't forget to make a hole for hanging before the Paperclay hardens. Brush with white glue and sprinkle with glitter.

Beaded Baubles

Beaded baubles are easily made by stacking graduated beads on a jewelry pin. Make a loop for hanging by bending the top of the pin with round-nose pliers. Paint and glitter.

Candy Canes

Twist together 2 small chenille stems. Use wire cutters to trim the cane to the desired size, and bend it into shape with your fingers.

Lollipops

Press a small ball of Paperclay into a semi-flat disc. Insert a toothpick for the stick and trim to the desired length with wire cutters. Allow the Paperclay to harden; then paint and glitter the lollipop.

Garlands

String small rocaille beads, separated by an occasional bugle bead, onto 32-gauge jewelry wire. The wire will give the strands more body and shape when you drape them onto the tree.

Star Topper

The star shape is easily found at a craft store as a premade bead, or you can make your own from Paperclay. Paint and glitter.

Other Miniature Ornaments

If you do not have enough time to craft all of the ornaments you need from scratch, purchase miniature ornaments and charms from a craft store and make them your own by repainting and adding glitter.

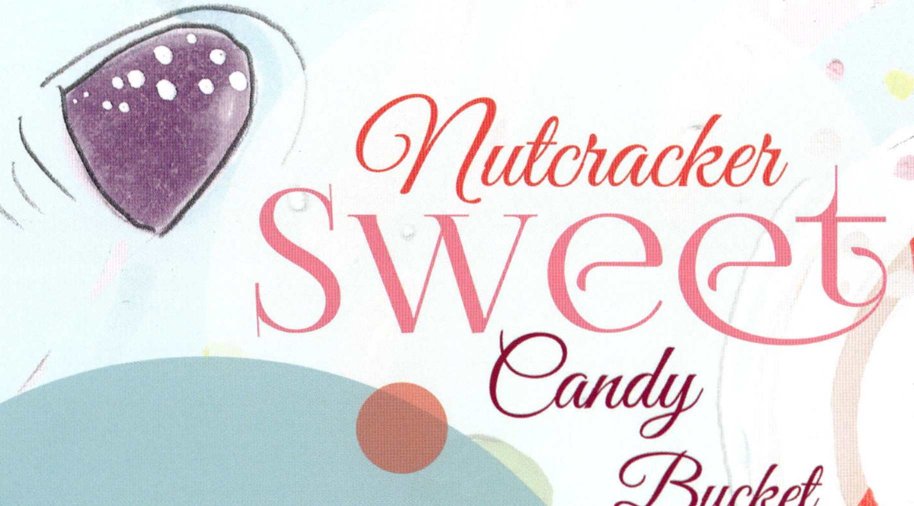

Nutcracker Sweet Candy Bucket

Ladies and gentlemen, carrots and beets,
come in from the cold, and put yourself in a seat.
What you're seeing today is a yummy holiday treat,
a feast for your eyes, not the kind your mouth eats.

This is the story about a nutcracker who's meek,
because his nut-cracking jaws are unfortunately weak.
When you look at his face and his hat that is dandy,
you would never suspect that he can crack only candy.

When his problem is mentioned,
he puts his head down and sobs,
because, no matter how handsome,
he can't do his life's job.

How could we help him . . . what words could we say?
Here's an idea—he could join the ballet!
There he would have no walnuts to crack.
He'd just lift ballerinas, fish-posed on his back.

Now he stands by Clara, sword-fighting the Rat King,
and waltzes with fairies wearing sugar-plummed wings.
This nutcracker now has a brand-new profession,
a moral for us all, about life's little lessons.

People now pay to see cracker's unusual talent,
chomping down on not nuts, but bonbons, how gallant!
If you're not good at one thing, give seven others a go,
and remember, you are the star, perfectly cast, in your own show!

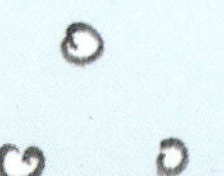

The Nutcracker Sweet

It wouldn't be Christmas without seeing a production of *The Nutcracker*, but this year you don't have to get dressed up and go to the ballet (although that's fun, too), because you can bring all your favorite characters to life right there on your craft table from materials you probably already have at home. So hurry and set the stage—the curtain on your production is getting ready to go up!

1 Make the bucket. Measure 2 inches on the cardboard tube with a ruler and use a pencil to mark it all the way around. Cut on the marked line with scissors or a craft knife.

2 Apply white glue around one edge of the cardboard tube. Wipe off any glue that may decide to drip down the sides.

3 Stick the tube to a flat piece of cardboard and allow it to dry completely.

4 Trim around the bottom edge with scissors, being very careful not to cut too close to the walls of the tube.

5 Copy the Nutcracker Face Template on card stock and cut out the eyes, nose, and mouth using a craft knife. Lay the template onto the side of the cardboard tube and use a pencil to trace the face.

6 Use a craft knife with a sharp blade to cut out the openings.

7 Brush the entire bucket with a coat of gesso or white acrylic paint and allow to dry.

8

9

10

11

8 Color block the inside and outside of the bucket. Set aside to dry completely.

9 Copy the nutcracker Face Insert Art on card stock and cut it out with scissors. Slide it into the bucket, centering the art in the openings, to check the fit. Trim as necessary. Remove the Face Insert Art from the bucket and apply white glue around the edges. Carefully re-insert it into the bucket and allow the glue to dry.

10 Copy the nutcracker Add-On Art on card stock and use scissors to cut out all the pieces. Use a pencil to trace the pattern pieces onto a flat sheet of cardboard and cut out using scissors or a craft knife. Attach the add-ons with white glue.

11 Add the details of the face with a small brush and acrylic paints.

12 Copy the Crown Art onto card stock. Cut out with scissors and glue inside of bucket as shown, using white glue.

13 Glue a handmade or purchased glittered star to the center of the front of the crown.

14 Use a hot glue gun to attach a strip of white marabou around the back of the head to create the hair.

15 Tuck a white feather plume behind the top of the glittered star and secure with white glue.

16 Add details to the crown with a small brush and acrylic paints.

17 Use a ⅛-inch hole punch to make a hole on each side of the bucket where the handle will be attached. Wrap an approximately 5-inch piece of 18-gauge floral stem wire with white floral tape and add stripes with acrylic paint. Allow to dry. Bend the wire into the shape of the handle by gently bringing the ends toward each other. Bend the ends of the wire inward. Insert the wire through the holes, as shown, and close the ends with needle-nose pliers.

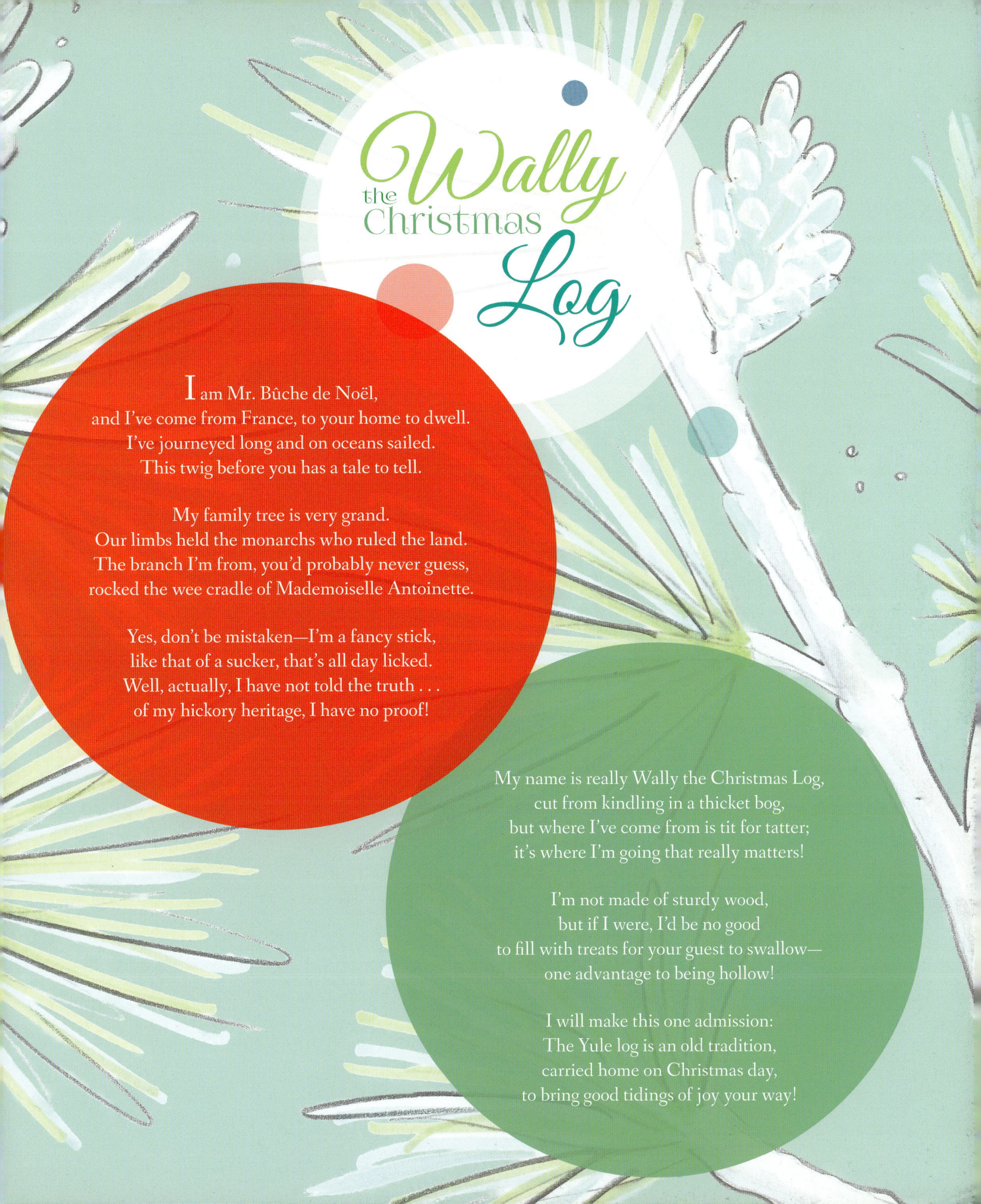

the Christmas Wally Log

I am Mr. Bûche de Noël,
and I've come from France, to your home to dwell.
I've journeyed long and on oceans sailed.
This twig before you has a tale to tell.

My family tree is very grand.
Our limbs held the monarchs who ruled the land.
The branch I'm from, you'd probably never guess,
rocked the wee cradle of Mademoiselle Antoinette.

Yes, don't be mistaken—I'm a fancy stick,
like that of a sucker, that's all day licked.
Well, actually, I have not told the truth . . .
of my hickory heritage, I have no proof!

My name is really Wally the Christmas Log,
cut from kindling in a thicket bog,
but where I've come from is tit for tatter;
it's where I'm going that really matters!

I'm not made of sturdy wood,
but if I were, I'd be no good
to fill with treats for your guest to swallow—
one advantage to being hollow!

I will make this one admission:
The Yule log is an old tradition,
carried home on Christmas day,
to bring good tidings of joy your way!

Wally the Christmas Log

There is nothing more exciting for me than going to an event during the holidays and getting a handmade party favor. Honestly, this rarely or never happens to me, but I can dream, can't I? Or better yet, I can make this a tradition at my house to show others how much fun it is to sit down for Christmas dinner and find, sitting on their dessert plate, a funny little log filled with candy that they can take home! Merry Christmas!

GATHER YOUR GLITTER, SCISSORS, AND GLUE. HERE'S EVERYTHING NEEDED FOR THIS MAKE AND DO!

Materials

- 2-inch-diameter cardboard tube
- Cardboard tube slightly smaller than the 2-inch tube
- Medium-weight cardboard
- White glue
- Face Template (page 181) (optional)
- Kitchen skewer
- Gesso (optional)
- Acrylic paints
- Textured snow paint (optional)
- Glitter
- Colored card stock scraps
- Red berries

Tools

- Ruler
- Pencil
- Scissors
- Craft knife
- Hot glue gun
- Photocopier (optional)
- Wire cutters
- ¼-inch-diameter dowel
- Paintbrushes

3

4

5

6

1 Make the log. Measure 4 inches in length on the 2-inch-diameter cardboard tube and use a pencil to mark all the way around. Use scissors or a craft knife to cut on the marked line.

2 Slide the smaller tube inside the log, as shown, to make sure it will fit.

3 Measure ¾ inch in length on the smaller tube and use a pencil to mark all the way around. Use scissors or a craft knife to cut on the marked line. This will become part of the cap.

4 Stand the log tube upright on a piece of medium-weight flat cardboard and trace around both ends. Use scissors to cut out both circles.

5 Carefully apply hot glue around one end of the log tube and attach one of the cardboard circles to close the end.

6 Make the removable cap for the other end of the log. Apply hot glue to the edges of the ¾-inch slice of smaller tube and center the remaining cardboard circle on it.

7 Insert the cap into the log to check the fit. It should be snug, but not too tight. If the fit is too loose, use white glue to apply a thin strip of paper around the outside of the cap.

8
9
10
11

8 Make the face. Start by drawing two eyes and a mouth in the center of the log with a pencil. You can freehand it or use the Face Template. Use a craft knife to cut a small X in the top of the log, as shown.

9 Use wire cutters to cut a 1-inch piece of kitchen skewer. Insert it through the X in the top of the log and secure it with hot glue.

10 Use a fully heated hot glue gun to squeeze circles of hot glue onto the end of the tube, creating the rings of the log. Repeat the circles on the cap as well. There is no right or wrong pattern, but it is important not to touch the glue once it is in place. Bubbles in the glue are fine, but you want to avoid strings of hot glue.

11 Being careful not to touch the hot glue rings on the end of the tube, add outlines of hot glue around the eyes and mouth. Leave a little distance between the glue and your pencil marks.

12 For this step, place the tube over a wooden dowel for holding. Fill the sides by making long lines of hot glue down the tube all the way around. Don't worry about making the lines straight. It will look more like a log if they wiggle a little. Allow the hot glue to cool completely.

13 Coat the entire log (inside and out) as well as the cap with gesso or white acrylic paint, and allow to completely dry.

12

13

14 Base coat the log and cap with brown acrylic paint. Allow to dry. Dry brush other colors over the brown to make it look more realistic. Use acrylic paint to add small detail lines to look like wood.

15 Color block the eyes and mouth and add shading. Use a small brush to add details to the eyes and mouth. Allow to dry.

16 Cover the top of the log with textured snow paint and sprinkle it with glitter. If snow paint is not available, you can apply a thick layer of white acrylic paint and sprinkle with glitter.

17 Finish it off with hand-cut card stock holly leaves and berries!

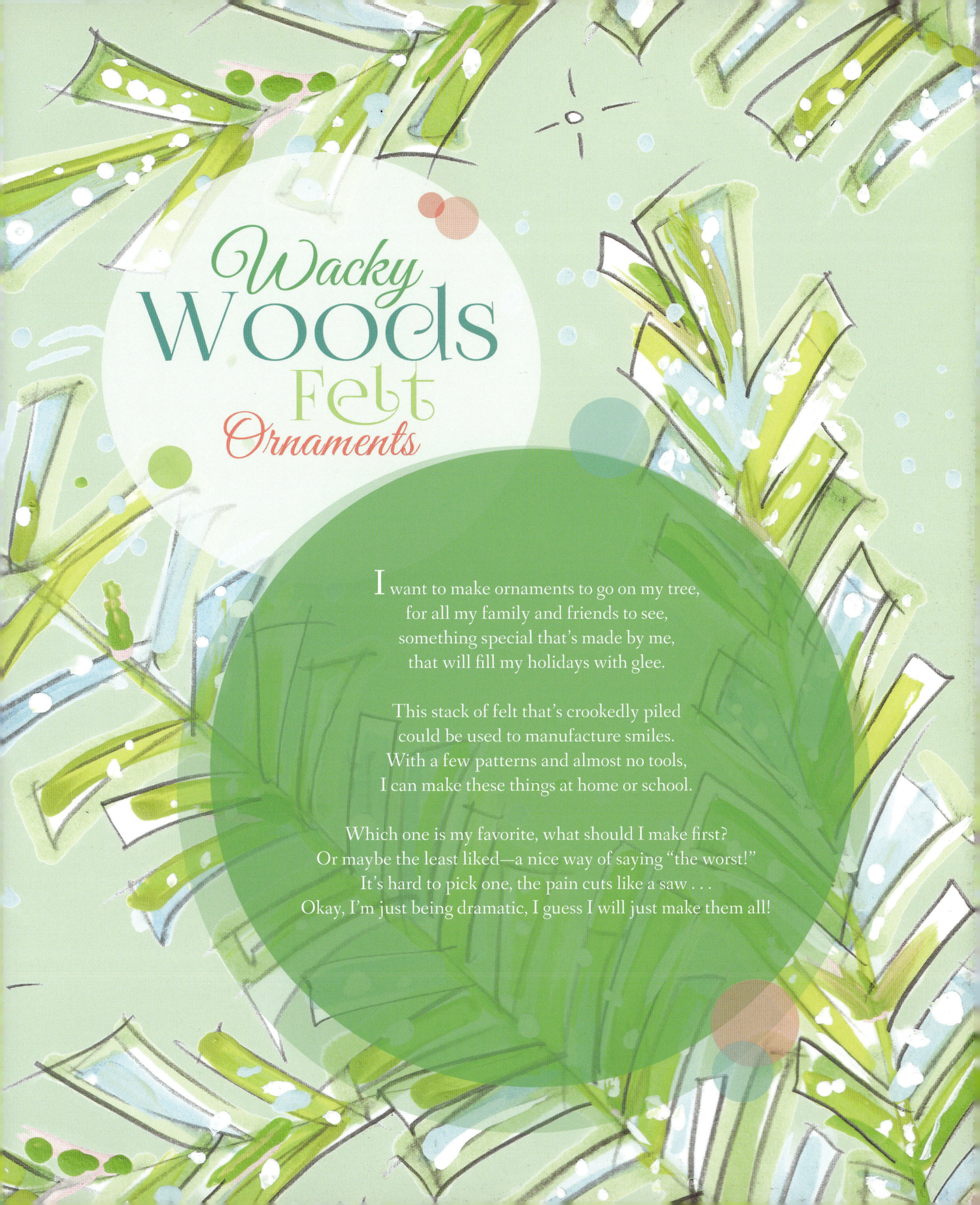

Wacky Woods Felt *Ornaments*

I want to make ornaments to go on my tree,
for all my family and friends to see,
something special that's made by me,
that will fill my holidays with glee.

This stack of felt that's crookedly piled
could be used to manufacture smiles.
With a few patterns and almost no tools,
I can make these things at home or school.

Which one is my favorite, what should I make first?
Or maybe the least liked—a nice way of saying "the worst!"
It's hard to pick one, the pain cuts like a saw . . .
Okay, I'm just being dramatic, I guess I will just make them all!

Wacky Woods Felt Ornaments

One of the easiest craft materials to work with, especially for a sewing project, is felt. Felt doesn't fray, and there are no messy strings or edges to hem each time you make a cut with the scissors, so it's almost like construction paper you can sew. Just cut out all the pieces, stack them up, add a few stitches, and these funny forest friends will be calling your tree their new home!

3

4

5

1 Copy the Wacky Woods patterns on card stock and cut out with scissors. Pin the pieces onto felt following the instructions on the pattern for the color and quantity needed for each piece. Use scissors to cut out all the pieces. Both the Mr. and Mrs. Happy Sap ornament styles are made following these steps.

2 Make the ornament. Start with the felt piece marked "Front" and center it on top of the character felt piece marked "Base." Attach the two pieces with a few drops of fabric glue to temporarily hold them together. Be careful not to put too much glue. You don't want it to show through the felt. Press flat with your hand.

3 Repeat this process with the layer of pieces as shown.

4 Continue layering with the final pieces.

5 Use black and white acrylic paints to add the black pupil and white glint to the eye.

6

7

8

9

6 Use the stitching guides on the pattern pieces and a craft needle threaded with embroidery floss to add the stitching details.

7 Add embellishments such as buttons, beads, and sequins with a needle and sewing thread.

8 Place the layered front piece on a square of felt sandwiching a small pile of felt scraps or fiber fill between the two to give stuffed dimension to the ornament once sewn.

9 Use a sewing machine or needle and thread to stitch all the way around the ornament. Cut out the ornament from the square of felt avoiding the stitches.

10 Use a needle threaded with embroidery floss to create a loop for hanging.

10

pinecone gnome

page 1

BACKPACK PATTERN—FRONT
Shown Actual Size

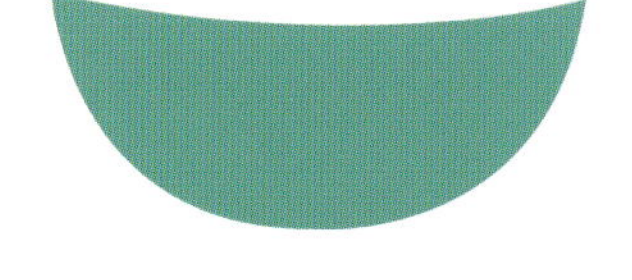

BACKPACK PATTERN—BACK
Shown Actual Size

HAT PATTERN
Shown Actual Size

glitter village

page 15

All House Pieces Shown Actual Size

INSIDE
CORNER BRACE
Cut 4

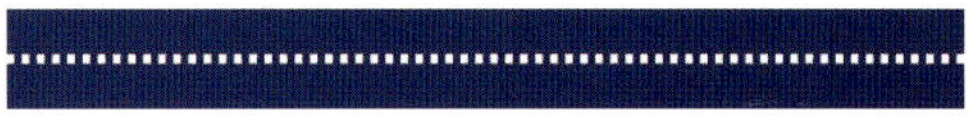

ROOF

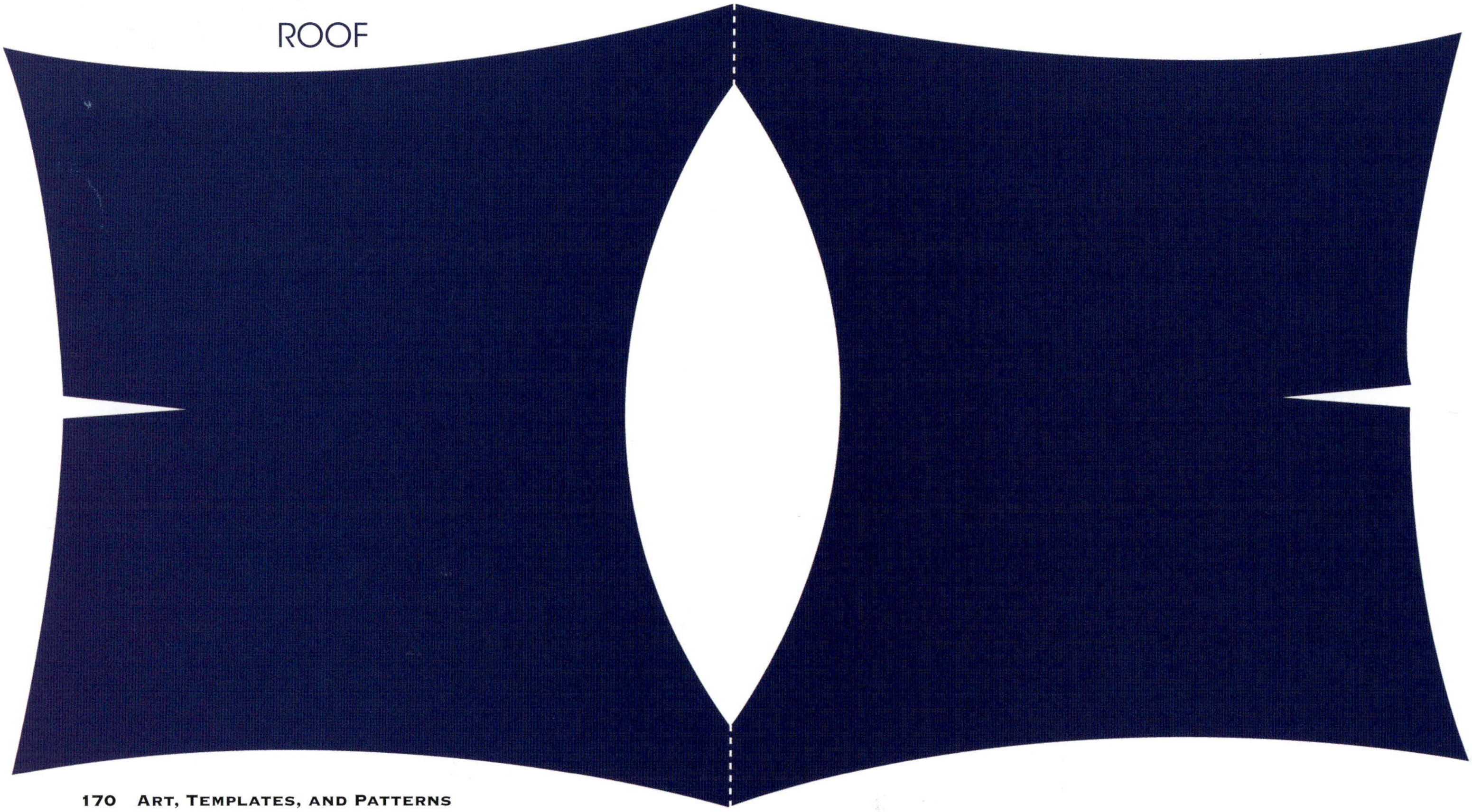

FRONT
CHIMNEY
FRONT
TAB
Cut 6
CHIMNEY
BACK
BACK

continued

All House Pieces Shown Actual Size
Score and fold along white lines

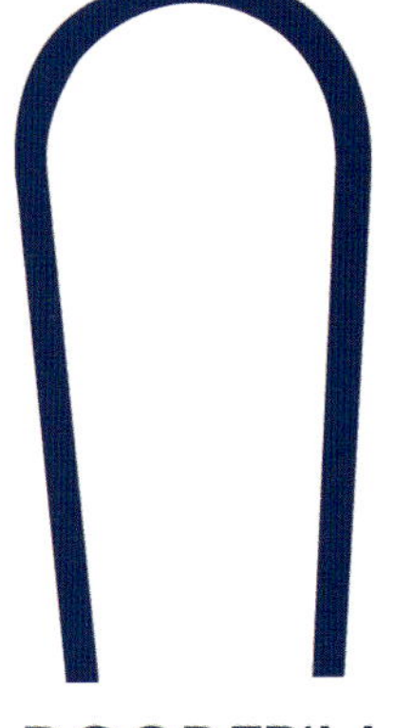

DOOR TRIM
Cut 1

CIRCLE WINDOW TRIM
Cut 3

DORMER WINDOW
Cut 2

LARGE WINDOW TRIM
Cut 2

SMALL WINDOW TRIM
Cut 2

DORMER WINDOW ROOF
Cut 2

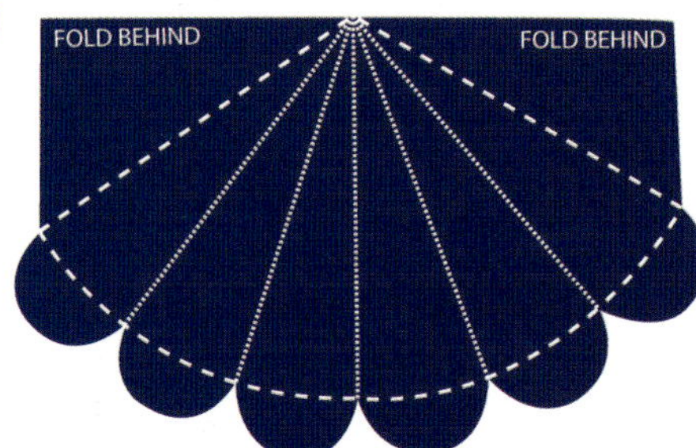

AWNING
Cut 1

AWNING SUPPORT
Cut 1

HOUSE CORNER TRIM
Cut 1

SMALL WINDOW BOX
Cut 2

LARGE WINDOW BOX
Cut 1

HOUSE CORNER TRIM BY CHIMNEY
Cut 3

CHIMNEY LEFT

CHIMNEY RIGHT

frosty folly on a swing

page 39

SWING FRAME WIRE TEMPLATE
Shown Actual Size

SWING FRAME SEAT TEMPLATE
Shown Actual Size

TAIL JACKET PATTERN
Shown Actual Size

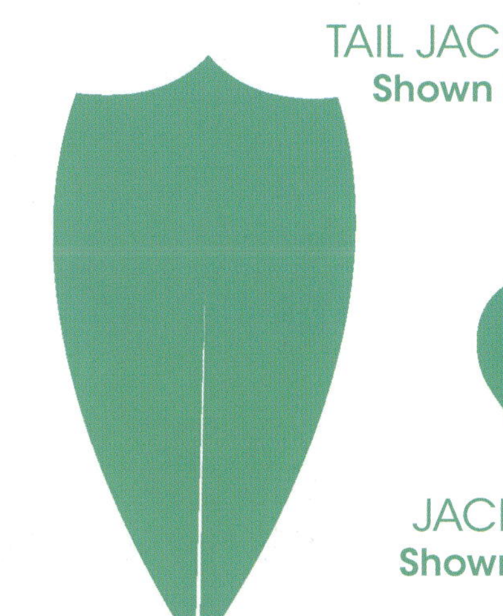

JACKET LAPELS
Shown Actual Size

HAT PATTERN
Shown Actual Size

glitzen the reindeer candy box

page 49

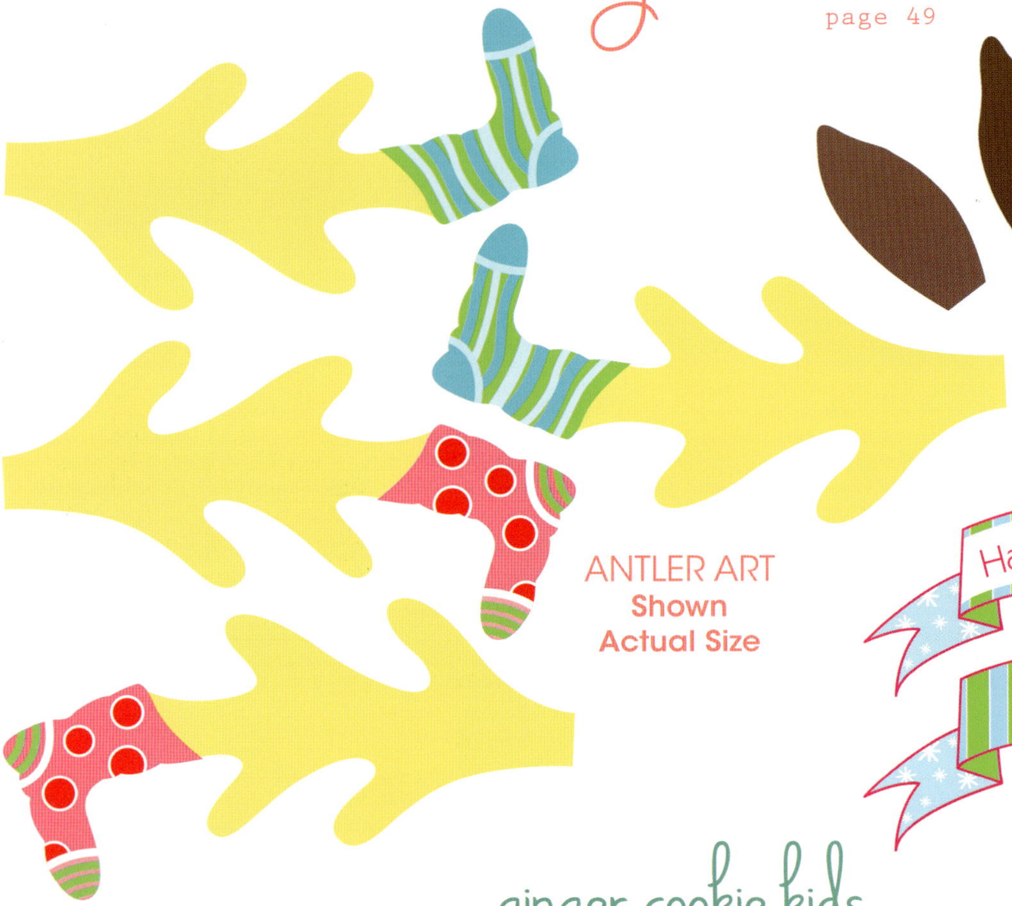

ANTLER ART
Shown Actual Size

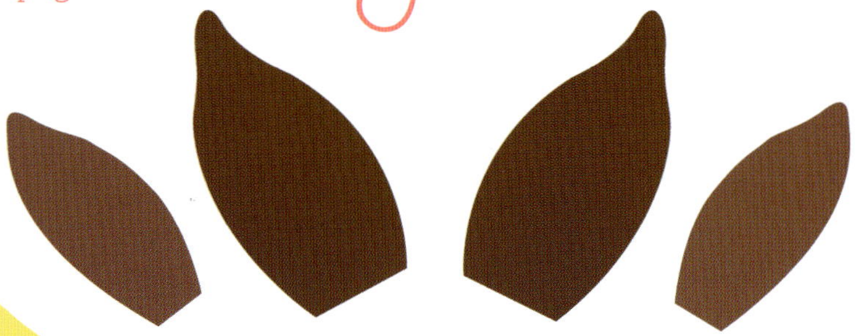

EAR PATTERN
Shown Actual Size

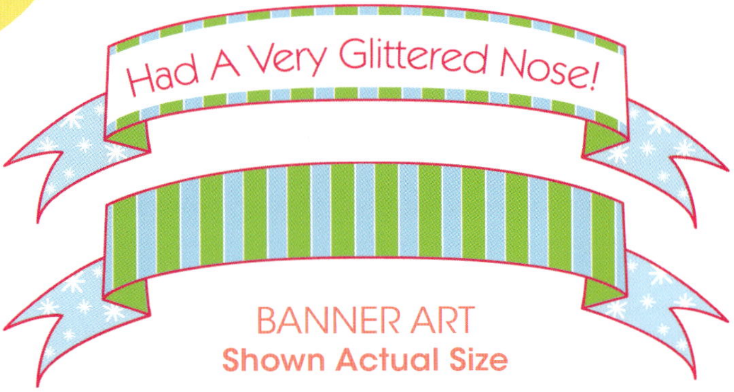

Had A Very Glittered Nose!

BANNER ART
Shown Actual Size

ginger cookie kids

page 57

GIRL DRESS

1

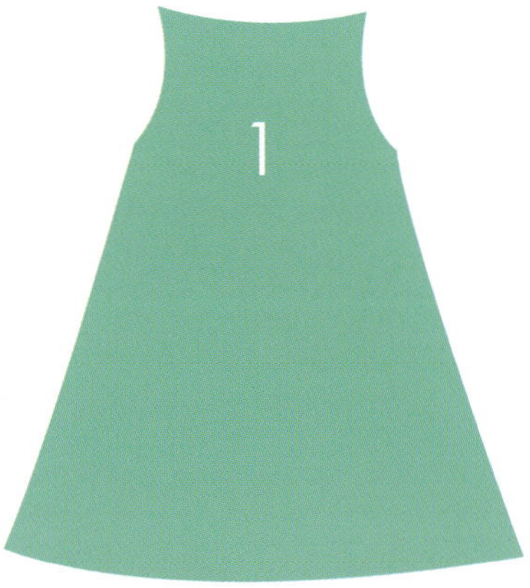

GIRL STYROFOAM PATTERN
1
1
BOY STYROFOAM PATTERN
BOY BODY
1
GIRL BODY
1

confectionery cone of candy

page 63

BANNER ART
Shown Actual Size

Oh So Sour!

Oh So Sweet!

CONE ART
Enlarge 200%

GLUE GLUE GLUE GLUE

CANDY AND LEMON ART
Cut 2
Shown Actual Size

FROSTING ART
Enlarge 200%

INSIDE

OUTSIDE

nutty as a fruitcake party hat

page 71

BANNER ART
Shown Actual Size

Nutty as a Fruitcake!

GLASSES ART
Shown Actual Size

jolly dolly holly wreath

page 89

WREATH PATTERN
Enlarge to 16" Wide

HOLLY LEAF PATTERN
Shown Actual Size

candy claus

page 101

HAT PATTERN
Shown Actual Size

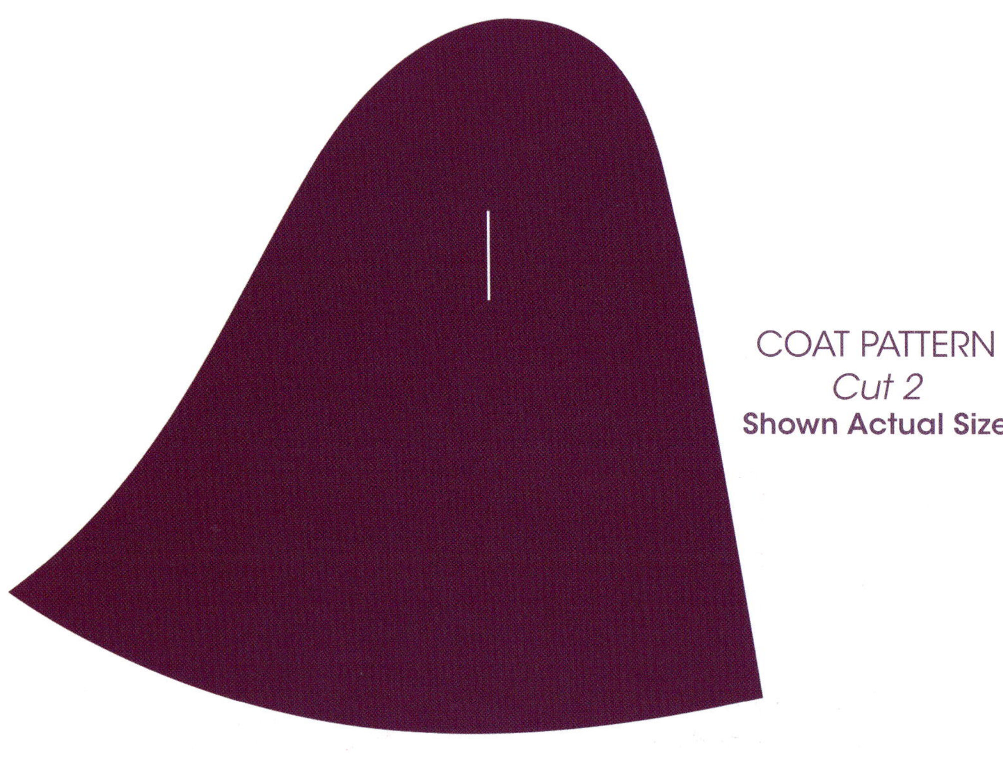

COAT PATTERN
Cut 2
Shown Actual Size

christmas in cupcake town

page 117

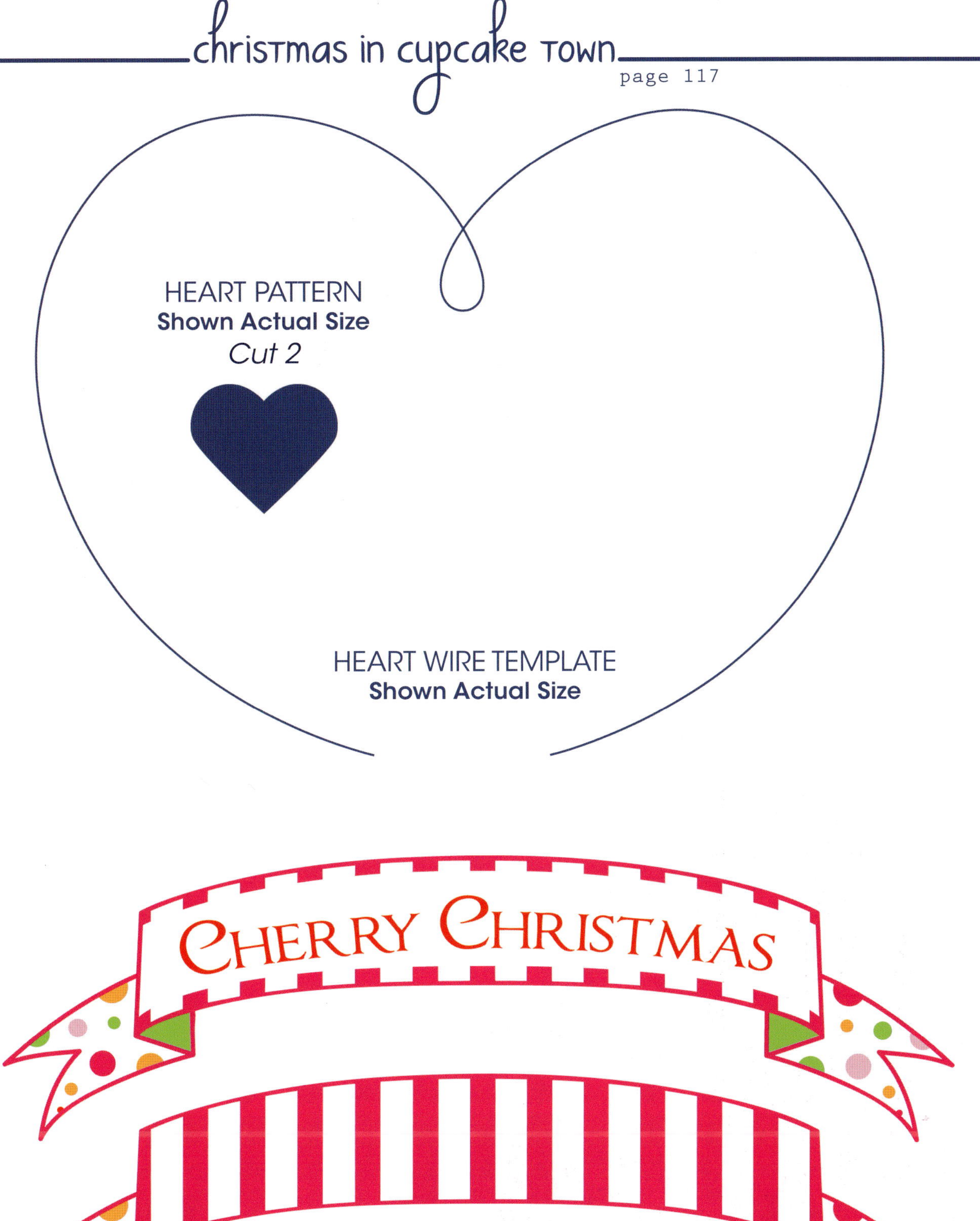

HEART PATTERN
Shown Actual Size
Cut 2

HEART WIRE TEMPLATE
Shown Actual Size

BANNER ART
Shown Actual Size

nutcracker sweet candy bucket

page 151

NUTCRACKER FACE TEMPLATE
Shown Actual Size

FACE ADD-ON ART
Shown Actual Size

HAIR ADD-ON ART
Shown Actual Size

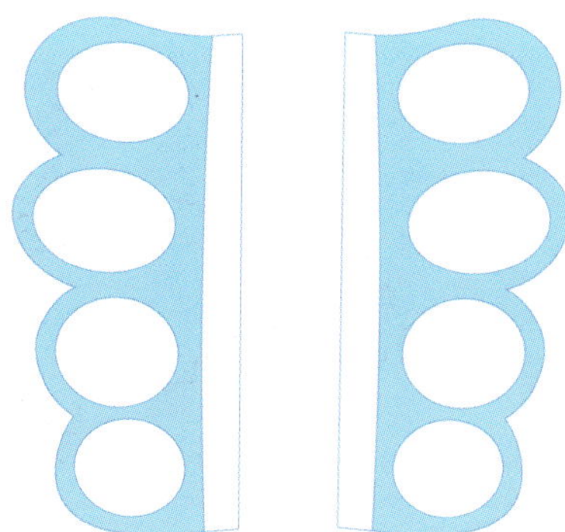

FACE INSERT ART
Shown Actual Size

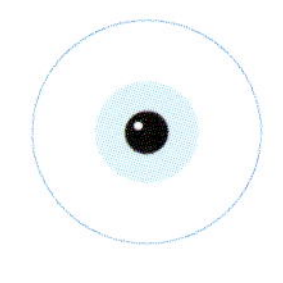

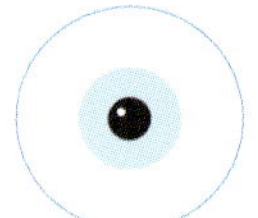

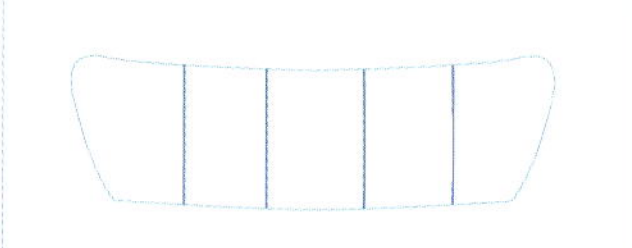

CROWN ART
Shown Actual Size

wally the christmas log
page 157
FACE TEMPLATE
Enlarge 200%
wacky woods felt ornaments
page 165
MRS. HAPPY SAP
Cut 1 of each piece
Enlarge 200%
FRONT
BASE
MR. HAPPY SAP
Cut 1 of each piece
Enlarge 200%
FRONT
BASE
Shown Actual Size
Shown Actual Size
Embroidery Guide in Blue
Embroidery Guide in Blue

Andrews McMeel Publishing, LLC
an Andrews McMeel Universal company
1130 Walnut Street, Kansas City, Missouri 64106

www.andrewsmcmeel.com

14 15 16 17 18 SDB 10 9 8 7 6 5 4 3 2 1

ISBN: 978-1-4494-1455-9

Library of Congress Control Number: 2011944595

www.glitterville.com

Behind the scenes of the Glitter Village shoot.

Fun Facts

Project glamours were all shot at Stephen's 110-year-old Edwardian-style house.

The final 20 projects were chosen from more than 100 of Stephen's favorite Christmas crafts.

Dolly Poulet laid an egg on the craft table during the making of her project.

Photos used in this book were edited down from over 45,000 shots.

Your make & do Merriment doesn't have to End

Just Flip this Book Over and Start Again!